Dedicated to

Our Parents

who were discerning enough
to recognize the evil in rock music
and who loved us enough
to withstand our reaction
as they led us to experience
true freedom

HOW TO CONQUER
THE ADDICTION OF ROCK MUSIC

CONTENTS

The Urgent Need To Understand This Addiction:

"He controlled us with rock music."

Surviving Branch Davidian Cult Member

New York Times News Service, Chicago Tribune, *April 20, 1993*

Reuters/Bettmann

WACO, Texas — The 30-minute inferno that consumed the Branch Davidian compound on Monday also swept away the lives of people drawn to Waco from as far away as Israel, Britain, Australia, New Zealand, and the Philippines.

The attraction: a man with a penchant for rock music, an occasional beer, and preaching Scripture with unwavering conviction.

CHARACTERISTICS OF ADDICTION

Rock music has been accepted as an amoral expression of individual taste; however, if it truly is an addiction, it must be treated as such with all the warnings and precautions that apply to any other addiction.

1 **The Tendency of an Addict to Deny His Addiction**
"I'm not addicted. I've quit many times."

2 **A Sacrifice of Relationships for the Addiction**
"If my parents won't let me listen to my music, I'll leave home."

3 **Compulsion to Engage in the Addiction at Any Time**
"This music gives me energy for whatever I do."

4 **A Practice of Secrecy Until Others Accept It**
"My parents don't understand my music, so I have to hide it."

5 **The Creation of an Appetite That Is Never Satisfied**
"I just need to hear the song one more time."

6 **Unusual Efforts to Feed the Addiction**
"I drove all over the city to find that new album."

7 **Using Any Money Necessary for the Addiction**
"Before long I amassed a small museum of rock music."

8 **A Readiness to Defend the Cause of the Addiction**
"You can't throw out rock just because some people overdo it."

9 **A Need to Involve Others in the Addiction**
"To reach teenagers we must use their language."

10 **A Reaction to Those Who Disagree With the Addict**
"You are being legalistic and judgmental of my music."

IS ROCK MUSIC ADDICTIVE?

The medical definition of an addiction is a "physical or psychological, or both, dependence"[1] on that which is not necessary for life. An addict is one who "devotes or surrenders himself to something habitually or obsessively."[2]

The characteristics of an addiction, listed on the previous page, are precise symptoms of millions of teenagers who expend great amounts of time, money, and effort to ensure that they have a continuous supply of rock music throughout their day.

The compulsive thoughts, moods, and behavior that rock music triggers in those who have surrendered to it and the incredible struggle that we face when trying to free ourselves from this force are further confirmations to us that rock music is addictive.

There are many researchers who could conduct extensive studies and surveys on rock music; however, in the final analysis, those who should have the most authoritative voice on the matter are those of us who listen to the music and whose lives are dramatically changed by what we hear.

In the summer of 1993, a music survey was conducted among 2,750 young people from all fifty states across America and from the countries of Canada, France, Mexico, New Zealand, the Netherlands, and Russia.[3]

These young people were asked the question, "Do you believe rock music can be addictive?" The results of this survey are presented on the following page. On pages 81–85, a psychiatrist explains why they responded this way.

"Nothing is more singular about this generation than its addiction to music."

— Dr. Allan Bloom
from his book, *The Closing of the American Mind*

Do Young People Believe That Rock Music Is Addictive?

In a survey of 2,750 young people,

99.3% said "Yes!"

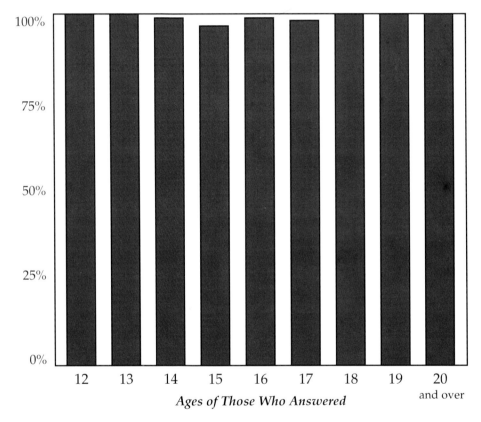

Ages of Those Who Answered

A survey on music was given to 2,750 young people between the ages of 12 and 26, from all 50 states and several foreign countries. The form was witnessed and signed by their parents. One of the questions asked if they believed that rock music was addictive. The results are shown in the graph above.[4]

"Can Christian Contemporary Music Cause Addiction?"

Matthew Mears (24) was introduced to Christian rock by a well-meaning friend who gave him a tape with only one "bad" song on it.

"One spring I had a job fixing up a house. The work required weeks of painting, wallpapering, and general repair.

"A well-meaning friend wanted to help me 'pass the time' while I worked, so he gave me his favorite tape of contemporary Christian music.

"I had never listened to this type of music before and was eager to be a part of whatever would strengthen my spiritual life. Most of the songs were familiar hymns that I had sung in church, but they had been 'livened up' to make them more exciting.

"There was only one song on the tape that had a strong rock beat. The more I heard this song, the more I wanted to listen to it. After several weeks, instead of listening to the entire tape, I would just listen to this song with the beat.

"As soon as the song was over, I would rewind the tape and listen to the same song again and again. Even when I wasn't playing this song, it seemed to keep playing in my mind. Each day as I put this tape on, I wanted to turn it up a little louder. Soon, I was playing it at full volume. It was as though I was addicted to this song.

"The words to the song were 'Shine down Your light on me....' It would seem that with the encouragement of this message, I would have become a greater witness for Christ. In reality, the contrary became true. Looking back, my spiritual life was taking a rapid downward turn that was characterized by compromise, apathy, and sensuality.

"The worst thing is that I didn't even notice the growing darkness that was overtaking my life. **The steady drone of the rock beat was a powerful anesthesia that deadened my spiritual senses and thus ushered in a host of tragic decisions.** Like a patient that is being operated on, I had no sense of spiritual pain.

"After I completed the house-repair job, I went on a trip to visit several friends. I was invited to do some things that I knew were wrong and of which my parents would not approve. Almost without thought, I chose to disobey my parents and the Lord. This was the first time in my life that I can remember ever willfully disobeying my parents. I am ashamed of the things in which I participated, and I only wish I could somehow remove the reproach that I brought to the name of Christ.

"Years have passed since that time, and God has shown me the deadly poison of the rock beat in any type of music. It took months of daily time in God's Word to regain the spiritual sensitivity that was lost during that season of my life. I grieve over the destruction that Satan brought to me through the rock beat. Please don't make the mistake I did by allowing this music into your life!"

Matthew Mears, Ohio

Note: Because the rock beat causes addiction, it makes little difference whether that beat is heard in Christian songs or secular songs. A slight rock beat that is introduced in music to those who have never heard it is a deceptive introduction to this addiction.

"How Did a Trusted Musician Start an Addiction?"

Sara Powers (19) traces the turning point in her life to the day she listened to a contemporary Christian tape at the age of twelve. The addiction that followed is typical of the experience of multitudes of young people.

"When I was twelve years of age, I purchased a tape that changed the course of my life. This tape was made by a popular Christian contemporary artist.

"Listening to this tape was the beginning of a pattern, or more accurately, an *addiction* of listening to rock music.

"Over a period of three years, I gradually went from contemporary Christian music to pop, light rock, and eventually, to hard rock.

"I would use rock music to entertain, get me excited, give me courage, and drown out my troubles. All of the things I used rock music for are also common reasons for alcohol or drug addiction, which is why I refer to it as an addiction in my life.

"The symptoms of my addiction were manifested in many ways: I withdrew from my family, became very rebellious, chose friends who listened to rock music, and spent hours by myself listening to rock music.

"Between the lifestyle that rock music leads into and the depressed, even suicidal thoughts that would occur as I listened to this music, I knew it was a bondage from which I needed to be freed. However, I did not have the power to do this. Each time I tried to break free, the next rock song I heard would pull me down again.

"Not until a year ago, when I heard that each rock song I listened to gave a piece of my soul to Satan, from which he could torment me, did I understand why rock music (and what it leads to) was so damaging in my life.

"I found that as I confessed listening to rock music as sin and now ask God to take back individual songs as I remember them, there is a complete release from the bondage and addiction to rock music. In place of rebellion and depression, God has given me freedom and joy!"

Sara Powers, Vermont

Christina Yerden (22) trusted the music of a Christian artist, but was led by that music into an apathy toward God.

A Further Witness of a Musician's Becoming a Wrong Influence

"I was born into a Christian family that loves music. I have enjoyed listening to and performing music since early childhood.

"My father never allowed us to listen to rock music. We listened only to Christian albums.

"When I was twelve, my father brought home an album of a Christian artist to whom we had listened for years; however, the music on this album was much more secular-sounding than on the previous ones.

"I remember feeling as though I was really getting away with something when I listened to this album, although my parents did not mind if I listened to it.

"It did not take me very long to become used to the backbeat* and sensual sound of this 'Christian' album, and soon it be-

*See page 95 for definition of *backbeat*.

11

came my favorite one. I would turn it on loud when no one else was home and dance around the living room.

"A year or so later, this same Christian artist came out with another album. This one had a much harder backbeat. Again, I was surprised that I was allowed to listen to such music, but quickly adapted to the harder beat.

"Along with the exposure I was getting at home, I was also listening to rock music at church with my friends in the youth group. The music I would hear in their cars got louder and harder. Often they would listen to secular rock.

"I experimented a little bit with secular rock, but I knew my parents would not approve of the words, so I discontinued that.

"In hindsight, I see now that it was also at twelve years of age (the same time I heard that first album) that I began to become apathetic about the things of God. He did not seem real to me anymore.

"I did not feel like spending time reading my Bible. As a result, I forgot about the holiness of God and what He requires of me. I began to compromise many of my standards, thinking that it was not 'that bad' to do so.

"When I hear rock music for very long, it desensitizes my spirit toward God. I would never have known it while I was listening to it, but I can see how it affects me when I am away from it for long periods of time.

"Believe me, I was one of the hardest people in the world to convince that the sound of rock music itself was wrong, but after not listening to rock music for awhile, it became obvious."

Christina Yerden, Washington

Note: "Praise music" that appeals to the emotions and physical senses rather than to the spirit violates the Biblical requirements of the true worship, because God is a Spirit and "*. . . true worshipers shall worship the Father in spirit and in truth: for the Father seeketh such to worship Him.*"[5]

The combining of worship and sensuality is not new. When the nation of Israel mingled with the heathen and learned their ways, they tried to adapt sensual Baal worship to their worship of God. This practice angered the Lord and brought judgment to the nation.[6]

"How Can Repulsive Music Cause Addiction?"

Melissa Perry (25) vividly remembers her first impression of rock music and how it gained a hold upon her mind by the influence of friends and repetition.

"As a child of ten years, I remember my classmates playing this music during lunch and turning up the volume as loud as possible whenever the teacher left the room. The music was repulsive to me. They asked me why I didn't like it and laughed at me because I was different.

"It wasn't hard to be different until my close friend began to play the music—someone I looked up to. On one occasion the music began to bother me so much I asked her to please turn it off. This request resulted in tears, arguments, and accusations of my being a 'goody-goody.'

"A few years later, I began dating a young man who liked rock music. He introduced me to contemporary Christian music, and I was curious. The words interested me, even though the music did not seem that great.

"Another friend had me listen to some of her Christian tapes. The lyrics were clever, so I did not pay much attention to the music, but I just listened with her, trying to catch the words.

"However, I did not realize what was really happening. I had attended several contemporary Christian concerts, and I remember one point when the music had a particularly dominant rock beat, the whole audience stood up, clapping with the music.

"I had a strange sense of wanting to participate and at the same time wanting only to observe what was going on. I felt foolish to be part of this music. My friend and I at first refused to follow the crowd, but everyone else was doing it, and it seemed awkward to be the only ones sitting. Eventually, we joined in.

"I began to listen to a Christian radio show late at night which played heavy Christian rock music. The music was still repulsive to me, but I was curious. Of course, I only turned it on after my parents went to bed.

"Soon after this time, I got a job where they played secular rock music all day long. I did not even think of asking them to turn it off. In fact, I thought I was not being affected by the rock music. I thought music was something I could control in my own mind. At the same time I wondered why I felt so far from God and confused in my spiritual walk.

"God used my parents to begin to show me that I should not listen to music which did not bring my heart closer to the Lord. I stopped listening to contemporary Christian music out of obedience, but I did not feel it had affected me that much. I did not correlate the new hunger and thirst I had for God with my recent obedience.

"Months later, after 'fasting' from this music, I heard some of the songs to which I had previously listened, and I was shocked by the worldly sound and felt sick inside.

"I had not realized the anesthetic properties of the rock beat. I had been introduced to it a little at a time, and my spirit was also dulled a little at a time, until I could no longer distinguish music that pleased God from that which was in rebellion against the purity of His Spirit."

Melissa Perry, Washington

Note: It is impossible to please God by adding sensual styles to spiritual songs, because *"the flesh lusteth against the Spirit, and the Spirit against the flesh: and these are contrary the one to the other: so that ye cannot do the things that ye would."*[7]

"How I Learned to Recognize the Rock Beat"

Kathy Voyer (23) is teaching thousands of children in the United States, Russia, Singapore, and other countries how to have Godly character. The amazing results which she is experiencing would all be lost if she had not recognized the addictive nature of rock music.

"I pressed my foot against the accelerator. The windows were rolled down, and the wind was rushing across my face. The car stereo was cranked up loud with one of my favorite Christian songs.

"'Feel the beat, feel the beat,' boomed this musical command. I listened to it; I embraced it; I obeyed it.

"I loved the beat. It was my comfort in sorrow, my solace in grief, my counselor in confusion. I was willing to stand against the disapproval of my parents, my pastor, and even some of my friends in order to satisfy my desire for the beat.

"This pursuit for the beat began when I was a little girl. My uncle, who is only six years older than I, would care for us while my parents were gone. He was my hero in every way. He would play 'hard rock' in his car.

"One afternoon we were stopped by a policeman and given a ticket because the music was so loud. My uncle's love for rock music progressed along with rebellion, drugs, suspension from school, thievery, and a police record.

"My uncle eventually moved away, but his music stayed with me. I began following in the same footsteps as my hero.

"I remember the first record I bought. It had pictures of prostitutes on the front. I noticed that the album covers of my favorite songs often depicted evil things. The beat seemed to increase my thirst for evil. My clothes, my habits, and my attitudes changed to reflect the rebellion within me.

"Shortly after my thirteenth birthday, my entire family responded to the message of salvation. Many changes took place as a result of our commitment to Jesus Christ. Alcohol bottles were emptied, books were burned, even my records and tapes were destroyed. I experienced great joy and freedom from the sins that had been controlling my life.

"However, it didn't take long for unresolved bitterness toward my mother to surface. I experienced anger and deep loneliness. Meanwhile, it seemed as if the rock beat was popping up everywhere. I tried to resist its influence, knowing the association that it had with my habits of the past, and yet I struggled to find something to fill my void.

"Then I was introduced to 'Christian rock' music as a means of evangelizing my unsaved friends. I was so excited, because I could find contemporary Christian artists that sounded like my old secular favorites. At first, I started with a mild beat, for fear of getting involved with rock music again. However, I was told by many respected Christians that it was the *lyrics* that made secular music wrong, not the tune.

"My old desire for 'the beat' was satisfied again, but the things it required of me waged a war within my soul. It seemed as though there was always a conflict between my family and me. Thoughts of suicide came to me during this period of time. I had a deep desire to follow the Lord, yet I could not understand why I had no victory in my daily life.

"I attended a seminar where I was challenged to dedicate my life to the Lord. This included yielding my rights in the areas of music, friends, and clothes. I confessed my hidden sins to my parents and asked them to forgive me for my rebellion.

"I purposed to seek their counsel for my decisions. When they started talking about 'my' music, I struggled to find where to draw the line between good music and bad music.

"The *Striving for Excellence* music course [IBLP] was presented in my Sunday school during that time. It gave examples of music that contained the rock beat. I laughed out loud as I heard these examples. I could not even hear the beat in those mild songs. Instead of having my questions answered about the rock beat, I was left with more questions.

"I prayerfully decided to go on a 'music fast.' I packed up all my questionable tapes and listened only to music that was clearly unquestionable. I began memorizing large portions of Scripture during this 'music fast'—something that I had had a difficult time doing before.

"Instead of falling asleep listening to music, I went to bed reciting Scripture. For the first time, I could see definite progress in my commitment to the Lord. Whenever I faced temptation, I would go to Scripture instead of my tape deck.

"After the music fast, I reevaluated my music tapes and was shocked to recognize the rock beat in many songs where I had never even heard it before.

"I then made it my goal to create a gap between the music to which I would listen and the music of the world, rather than seeing how close I could come to the line. This gap was created by taking steps to regain the 'ground' in my soul that I had given to Satan through wrong music. Now I am so glad that I am finally free!"

Kathy Voyer, California

Note: If you are unable to carry out a "fast" from rock music for at least a month, it would confirm that you are addicted to it. The Apostle Paul stated that *"all things are lawful for me, but I will not be brought under the power of any."*[8] He stated that he kept his body under the strictest discipline, lest having preached to others, he himself should be a castaway.[9]

Nick Lancette (26) has provided leadership and training for hundreds of Russian young people who have recently come to Christ. He has observed firsthand in the Russian culture the devastation that rock music is having in that nation.

"How Christian Rock Was No Alternative to Secular Rock"

"From inside my house, I could hear the music playing outside. I knew my friends had arrived to take me to football practice.

"As we drove, I could hardly hear myself speak due to the volume of the rock music. It seemed to create a wild, unrestrained atmosphere that drowned out the 'voice' of better judgment. At the time, I wondered how my friends could be so committed to such obnoxious music, yet I did not realize that there were similar desires developing in my own life.

"Although I did not care for their brand of rock music, I began to listen to my own. I believed that it was simply a form of entertainment. However, I did not recognize the path of destruction on which it was leading me.

"Many times I would listen to my favorite songs over and over again, and I was unconsciously developing a habit of worshiping sensuality. This stirring up of lust within me began to corrupt the thoughts of my heart and weaken my natural inhibitions. Soon these new fleshly values became the basis of many decisions in my life.

"As my thoughts were held hostage by the relentless desires engendered through this 'innocent' entertainment, I began to realize the grave danger in which I had brought my spiritual life. About this time, I heard some messages that warned about the evils of rock music, and I knew I needed to make commitments to stop listening to and even desiring this sort of music.

"I did so, but I struggled to follow through on my commitments. I still found myself battling with inordinate desires that were difficult to overcome. It seemed that the more I struggled, the more I longed to gain victory.

"My spiritual drives were growing all the time, yet I seemed unable to shake the wicked ways and thoughts of my flesh. Like a rubber band stretched tightly, I felt the tension of strong, conflicting desires between the flesh and the spirit. I knew that one would eventually have to let go.

"The contemporary Christian music to which I began listening was also powerless to break the strongholds which rock music had entrenched in my soul.

"Not long after this, the Lord gave my father and me the opportunity to spend some time together at a seminar in Biblical principles. The truths of God's Word which were presented began to confront the false ideas I had accepted, and by agreeing with God, I began to tear down the 'strongholds' in my soul.

"My spirit confirmed all that I heard through the week, and my father and I had terrific times of discussing all that the Lord was teaching each of us. This was the beginning of new spiritual growth in my life and a strengthened relationship with my father, which afforded new ability to stand alone as a teenager."

Nick Lancette, Montana

Note: Nick's experience with rock music confirms the truth of the following quotation: "[Sin] is a monster of such awful mien, That to be hated needs but to be seen, But seen too oft, familiar with face, We first endure, then pity, then embrace."[10]

"How Christian Rock Contributed to Delinquency"

David Hill (26) can now evaluate the events that took place during his teenage years, as he is free from his former bondage. David gave this testimony to a gathering of Christian leaders on March 30, 1992.

"When I was a young teenager, there was a clear distinction between the world's music and God's music.

"The world's rock music appealed to my flesh, and in my spirit I knew I could not listen to it because the words were wrong and the role models were bad. I had Godly parents who taught me that the world's music was not right.

"It was just about that time that we started having a new kind of music. When I got this new Christian music, it didn't sound too bad, and the words were good, so I started listening to it. At first, it was only a little different—it was a little new and had a little bit of the world's sound.

"However, it got progressively more and more like the world's music. Eventually, it sounded exactly the same, so I reasoned, 'Why not listen to the world's music? After all, the only difference is the words.'

"What I did not understand, however, was that the music did a lot more than just carry the words. It stirred up sensuality in me that I didn't know how to control. When I was fourteen or fifteen years old, this music stirred up desires which I had no ability to suppress or deal with. I became a slave to immorality.

"It wasn't a question of whether the music was right or wrong, because that did not matter to me. Somebody could come to me and say, 'This worldly music that you have now given yourself over to is wrong.' However, I could not agree with them, because I HAD to listen to it. I had no choice.

"Nevertheless, I still didn't understand that the music and my failure morally, my failure with purity, were bound together. I would struggle; I would pray about my moral failures: 'Lord, I commit myself to You. I dedicate myself to You. I give this area of my life to You. And I claim victory in You.' Nevertheless, I did not get rid of the music, and no sooner would I finish praying and I would be right back into my sins. I could not get away.

"After years of rebellion and doing things that were very damaging to myself and to those around me, I finally got back under my parents' authority *and* God's design for music.

"I saw that rock music, rebellion, and immorality were hooked together, and that only when you get rid of the wrong music can you get rid of the immoral desires and wrong feelings to which I was in bondage.

"As I talked with others about music, they tended to argue, just like I did. However, when it comes right down to it, I can look them in the eye and say, 'Are you experiencing victory in your life morally?' After talking to *hundreds* that listen to this music, not one has said to me 'Yes,' truthfully 'Yes.'

"I bring you a plea, a cry from my generation, from the generation that was brought up in this and through this music, and for the next generation that is coming along. **<u>STOP</u>** this music. HELP US! Or we will find a moral decay like we have never known—like what we are seeing develop right now."

David Hill, Oklahoma

Note: Contributing to the delinquency of a minor is a criminal offense in every state. Illinois law reads, "Any person who knowingly or willfully causes, aids, or encourages any boy or girl to be a delinquent child, or who knowingly or willfully does acts which directly tend to render any such child so delinquent is guilty of the Class A misdemeanor of contributing to the delinquency of children."[11] Based on the witnesses of these young people, any promotion of rock music carries the liability of willful criminal activity against those under 18 years of age.

How Christian Leaders Responded . . .

The testimony you have just read was given to a large group of Christian leaders on March 30, 1992. These leaders represented ninety Christian organizations. They were meeting together to coordinate their work in the former Soviet Union.

This unprecedented conference was led by Dr. Bruce Wilkinson and hosted at the Moody Bible Institute in Chicago. After David and several other young people gave their testimonies on the dangers of rock music, leaders stood to affirm the truth of what we said.

This discussion prompted Dr. Wilkinson to remark, "Young people, don't forget what you have just experienced. . . . Sharing your burden with people who love the Lord has an impact."

Dr. Bill Bright, President of Campus Crusade for Christ, suggested that a resolution be made that no rock music would be brought to Russia through the CoMission association. Then these leaders stood together for a solemn time of prayer led by Dr. Wilkinson. Here is his prayer:

A Solemn Commitment Before God
Not to Take "Christian Rock" into Russia

"Our Father in Heaven, we do bow before You. You know how we struggled for hours about this; trying to seek Your Face—not desiring, Lord God, to quench Your Spirit. We sense Your guidance tonight, and we do bow before You and praise You. There is no offense taken of any of us here about this issue. This is truth, and the truth sets us free. We have been freed.

"We hereby commit together under Your hand that at no time, knowingly or when we do find out, will the CoMission be involved in any Christian rock or secular rock. We bind together underneath Your authority, Lord God, and ask for Your blessing upon our commitment tonight. Amen."

An Urgent Message to Christians, From the Former. . .

Persecuted Church in Russia

Vasilij Ryzhuk *(left)* spent eleven years in a prison camp for his faith, and Peter Peters *(right)* was imprisoned fifteen years. The Communists used rock music day and night to try to break down their faith. Can you imagine how they feel when Christian groups bring the same rock music to their country? They are pictured here signing this statement.

"For thirty years we have suffered intense persecution, and now freedom is bringing another great harm to our churches. This damage is coming from the Christians in America who are sending rock music and evangelists accompanied by rock bands.

"Our young people do not attend these meetings because we have all committed not to participate in secular entertainment. This is a great burden on our hearts.

"Many come with Bible in hand and rock music. We are embarrassed by this image of Christianity. We do not know what words to use in urging that this be stopped. We abhor all Christian rock music coming to our country.

"Rock music has nothing in common with ministry or service to God. We are very, very against Christian Americans bringing to our country this false image of 'ministry' to God. We need spiritual bread—please give us true bread, not false cakes. It is true that rock music attracts people to the church, but not to Godly living.

"We were in prison for fifteen years and eleven years for Christ's sake. We were not allowed to have Christian music, but rock music was used as a weapon against us day and night to destroy our souls. We could only resist with much prayer and fasting.

"Now, we have a time of more openness, and we are no longer taken to prison. However, now it is Christians from America who damage our souls. We do not allow this music in our church, but they rent big stadiums and infect teenagers and adults with their rock music.

"We, the leadership and congregations of the Unregistered Union of Churches, the former Persecuted Church, have made an agreement to not allow rock music in our churches. We urge you to join with us, and we advise you to remove rock music from America, and certainly do not bring it to our country.

"Do not desecrate our teenagers with it. Even the unbelievers recognize it is unholy music and they cannot understand how American Christians can be so much like the world. We can give you the conclusion that after Russian unbelievers have attended these rock concerts where Christ's Word was preached, the people were very disappointed and disillusioned with Christianity.

"We call this music from hell. We urge all Americans to stop giving money for the organization of such concerts in Russia. We want only traditional Christian music in our churches. This is the unanimous decision of all our leaders."

Peter Peters, Head of the
Unregistered Union of Churches
Moscow, Russia, November 1991

Vasilij Ryzhuk, Elder of the
Unregistered Union of Churches

A CONFIRMING WITNESS

On July 10, 1993, Sergei Andropov, Member of the Russian Parliament and Deputy Chairman of the Committee for Social Policies, read this letter. He affirmed the growing problem of rock music in his nation and wrote the following statement:

"I would like to join the statements made by these Russian church leaders. Almost every priest in the Russian churches will tell you that rock music is from the devil, not from God. To use rock music to bring young people into the church is to turn them away from their search for true faith in God."

Sergei Andropov, Member of the Russian Parliament
Deputy Chairman of the Committee for Social Policies

Two weeks later, at the urging of the Russian Orthodox Church, the Russian Parliament passed legislation restricting Western missionaries from coming into their country.

How To Conquer
THE ADDICTION
OF ROCK MUSIC

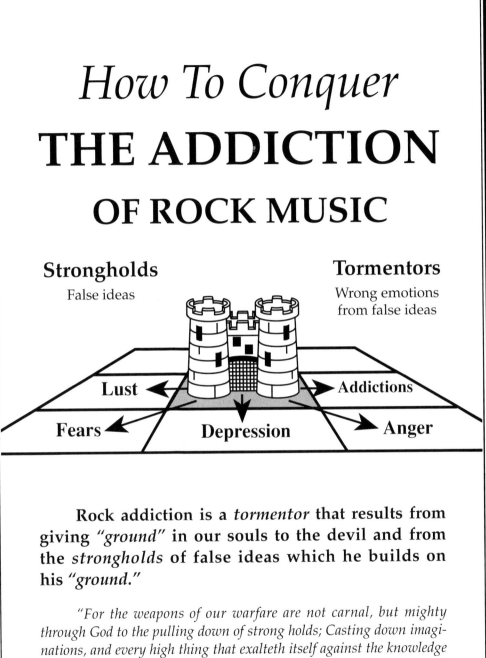

Strongholds

False ideas

Tormentors

Wrong emotions
from false ideas

Lust ← → Addictions

Fears ← Depression → Anger

Rock addiction is a *tormentor* that results from giving *"ground"* in our souls to the devil and from the *strongholds* of false ideas which he builds on his *"ground."*

"For the weapons of our warfare are not carnal, but mighty through God to the pulling down of strong holds; Casting down imaginations, and every high thing that exalteth itself against the knowledge of God, and bringing into captivity every thought to the obedience of Christ" (II Corinthians 10:4–5).

HOW ADDICTION OCCURS

When we were addicted to the rock beat, we could not be convinced by any argument that it was wrong. Even though down deep in our hearts we may have known it was not right, we resisted any Scripture or logic that would make us feel guilty, and we would look for reasons to justify the music.

It was only as the devastating symptoms of rock addiction increased that we began to seriously wonder if there was some connection between feeling distant from God, a weakness to temptation, and the music to which we were listening. As in other addictions, by the time we acknowledged concern about the damaging results of this habit, it was too late to change.

Only now do we realize what was happening in our souls as we listened to each rock song.

1 *It Begins With Surrendered "Ground."*

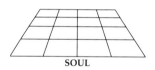

SOUL

The soul can be pictured as being a checkerboard with areas of jurisdiction ("ground"). When all the areas of the soul are under God's control, we experience inward peace and joy. However, if we surrender any of these areas of the soul to Satan, he takes charge of them and begins robbing us of the resources and potential of our lives.

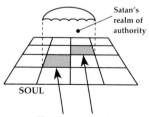

Satan's realm of authority

SOUL

Thoughts or acts of bitterness, greed, or immorality (can be caused by rock music)

We surrender "ground" to Satan in three primary ways: bitterness, greed, and immorality. In the fourth chapter of Ephesians these root sins are defined, and we are then warned not to go to bed angry, because doing so will give place ("ground") to the devil.[12]

2 *It Is Based on "Strongholds."*

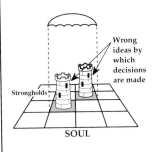

Wrong ideas by which decisions are made

Strongholds

SOUL

Once an area of the soul is under Satan's jurisdiction, he builds "strongholds" on it.

A "stronghold" is a false idea, an unscriptural conclusion, or an erroneous presupposition. It is an inaccurate frame of reference from which we make wrong decisions. It is these "strongholds" that God wants us to tear down with His truth.

". . . The weapons of our warfare are not carnal, but mighty through God to the pulling down of strong holds; Casting down imaginations, and every high thing that exalteth itself against the knowledge of God, and bringing into captivity every thought to the obedience of Christ."[13]

3 *It Is Established by Iniquity.*

Whenever we do things that are not directed by God, we commit iniquity, even though the things we do may look good to those around us.

Jesus said that many would come to Him one day and say, *". . . Lord, Lord, have we not prophesied in thy name? and in thy name have cast out devils? and in thy name done many wonderful works?"* He will say to them, *". . . Depart from me, ye that work iniquity."*[14]

It is amazing to consider that preaching, or casting out demons, or doing wonderful works could be iniquity. Yet, whatever is not done by the direct will of God is described in Scripture as *iniquity*.

Jesus stated that He did nothing of His own will, but only the will of His Heavenly Father.[15] When we say or do something based on the false ideas of Satan's strongholds, we can be sure that it is iniquity. We may be able to justify it and defend it with our own reasoning, but it is still iniquity.

4 *It Is Recognized Through "Tormentors."*

The consequences of committing iniquity are destructive emotions such as fears, doubts, depression, lust, and anger. Further tormentors are the pain of broken relationships and the loss of valuable resources.

The purpose of these tormentors is to exert pressure on us. To be tormented is to have a mental or physical affliction imposed upon us from a source outside our control. Torments are caused at the will of the tormentor and are continuous or can be sporadic—coming at any time.

Torments dominate the mind and emotions of the one being tormented. They drain the person of his vitality and the potential of his life. They demand his attention and rob him of peace and freedom. When a person believes that there is no escape from his torments, he may try to accept them and adapt to them, but there will always be the hope or longing to be free.

The Development of Rock Addiction

1	2	3	4
When we are bitter, greedy, or immoral, we give areas of control in our souls to the devil.	Satan brings wrong ideas into these surrendered areas of the soul, such as "music is amoral."	These false ideas cause us to make incorrect decisions; i.e., "I will listen to rock music."	Destructive emotions and relationships develop from our wrong actions.
"Ground"	*"Strongholds"*	*"Iniquity"*	*"Tormentors"*

How Strongholds Produce Tormentors

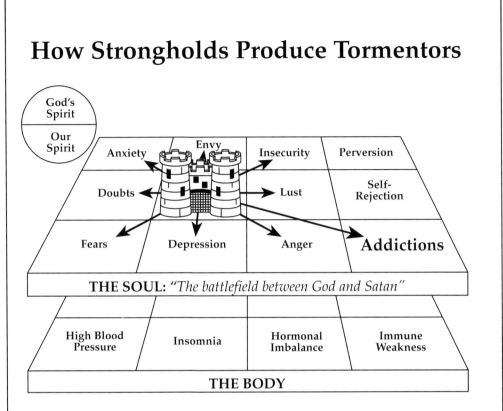

God's Spirit

Our Spirit

Envy

Anxiety

Insecurity

Perversion

Doubts

Lust

Self-Rejection

Fears

Depression

Anger

Addictions

THE SOUL: *"The battlefield between God and Satan"*

High Blood Pressure

Insomnia

Hormonal Imbalance

Immune Weakness

THE BODY

At salvation, God's Spirit enters our spirit, and we are born again. Then we have the ongoing need to transform our soul. When a person gives way to anger, greed, or immorality, he gives jurisdictional area ("ground") to Satan in his soul. Satan then builds his strongholds of false ideas on this "ground," which become the basis of wrong decisions. Once wrong ideas are carried out in word or deed, tormentors afflict other areas of the soul.

How Rock Music Becomes a Tormentor

The testimony of Misty is typical of thousands of young people: "When I got angry at my parents for not giving me my way, I went to my room and turned on my rock music. The music told me I did not need my parents and that what I want to do is my own business. I began making my own decisions against my parents' wishes and got into a lot of trouble with wrong friends, drugs, and addiction to rock music and rap."

— *Misty West, 14, Tennessee*

STEPS TO REGAIN "GROUND"

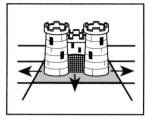

Before we can conquer rock addiction, we must confess our sins and ask God to regain the "ground" that was given to Satan through bitterness, greed, or immorality. Every time a rock song comes to your mind, trace it to surrendered "ground" and follow these steps.

1 *Confess Anger, Deception, and Lust to God.*

If there was an evening that you got angry at one of your parents, went to your room and turned on the rock music which you knew your parents did not like, and went to sleep angry, then according to Scripture, you gave "place" to the devil.[16]

God promises that *"if we confess our sins, he is faithful and just to forgive us our sins, and to cleanse us from all unrighteousness."*[17] This verse is written to believers. Notice that we are not to confess that we have sinned or that we are sinners, but we are to confess specific sins. We gave away "ground" to Satan sin-by-sin, now we must take back that "ground" confession-by-confession.

2 *Claim the Blood of Christ for Each Sin.*

Believers are cleansed from all sin at salvation.[18] Further sins give Satan undeserved authority in the soul, but we can overcome Satan by Christ's blood and by our testimony about His blood. *". . . They overcame him [Satan] by the blood of the Lamb, and by the word of their testimony. . . ."*[19]

3 *Audibly Ask God to Regain Lost "Ground."*

It is important to verbally ask God to take back "ground" we gave to Satan by our sins. We are not able to take "ground" back ourselves, but God can. *"He restoreth my soul. . . ."*[20] Sincerely ask, **"God, would You take back the 'ground' I gave to Satan with the sin of _____."**

Further Steps to Take:

4 *Confess Secret Sins to Your Parents.*

Having confessed sins to God, it is also important to tell those who are responsible for our spiritual welfare, such as parents. Many do not find freedom until they humble themselves in this way. *"He that covereth his sins shall not prosper, but whoso confesseth and forsaketh them shall have mercy."*[21]

5 *Tear Down Every Stronghold With Truth.*

Every rock song we accepted in our minds contains strongholds of false ideas. Each one must be cast down and replaced with specific truths from the Bible. Develop disciplines such as Scripture memorization, daily Bible reading, and meditation on God's Word, and *". . . receive with meekness the engrafted word, which is able to save your souls."*[22]

6 *Cleanse Your Home of All Rock Music.*

". . . Make [no] provision for the flesh, to fulfill the lusts thereof."[23] Any rock music or materials in your home will bring defeat. The Christians of Ephesus showed their repentance by burning all their evil books and materials.[24] In Deuteronomy 7:25 God commanded to burn with fire the graven images that are worshiped by the world.

7 *Replace Rock Music With Godly Music.*

The best way to get darkness out is to let the light in. If we fail to replace evil music with good music, Satan will fill the void with even more destructive addictions. If you cannot locate melodious music, we would be happy to help you. (See page 95.)

8 *Repeat These Steps for Further "Ground."*

Each time you remember a rock song, confess it as iniquity, claim the blood of Christ, and ask God to take back the "ground" given Satan and to tear down the strongholds which Satan built in your soul. Do not stop this process until all the "ground" is regained.

How Listening to "Christian Rock" Gave "Ground" to Satan

Ruthie Fritsch (21) reveals what happened to her as a lead singer in a contemporary Christian music group.

"All my life I have had a strong desire to follow the Lord, whatever the cost. I daily delighted myself in memorizing Scripture, praying, and encouraging others.

"When I was in the sixth grade, my best friend introduced me to 'Christian rock' music. At first I didn't enjoy it, because it gave me a deep unrest in my spirit, but it didn't take long for me to become accustomed to it. Soon it became a regular part of my life, and I felt that I almost couldn't live without it.

"This music began to change me into a self-seeking, sensual person. It drove a wedge between me and my parents, contributing to deep bitterness in my family. The music also turned my focus to things of the world.

"By the time I reached high school, I was desperately seeking a new way of life. I wondered, 'Is there fulfillment in *anything*? How can I get closer to Christ? I know He is the answer, but *how* do I know Him?'

"My youth leaders directed me to heavier 'Christian rock' music while at the same time teaching me the importance of reading the Bible. With a combination of the Scriptures and rock music, I was living by what I now see was my own religion—the 'Sensual Gospel.'

"Using my own definition of *grace,* I felt free to fulfill my fleshly lusts. I wanted to know God, but on *my* terms. My friends and I worshiped with 'Christian rock' music, we drove with

'Christian rock' music, and we defrauded each other with 'Christian rock' music. It controlled my life.

"My life-long desire had been to go to the mission field, so my parents helped me join a missions organization when I graduated from high school. I thought I had finally *achieved* my aspirations in the Christian life.

"However, my struggle only intensified as I became a lead singer for a 'Christian rock' evangelistic band in Europe. I soon realized that not much had changed in my life. I still had strongholds of sensuality, and I could not gain victory. I deeply desired to know God, but there were so many walls I could never get through.

"While our group was singing one night in Romania, God began to show me the destruction that this 'Christian rock' music caused. I had just finished singing, and my friend started to give a testimony of what God had done in his life.

"I looked out over the crowd and saw confusion on almost every face. They hadn't understood the words of the songs— only the music—and the music carried a much different message than the words of my friend's testimony. The people went home confused. I came back from Europe disillusioned and questioning that for which I had given the previous two years. My life was steeped in iniquity (doing 'good' things in my own strength that are not the will of God).

"Soon after my return, I was introduced to a man my father respected, and he encouraged me to dedicate every area of my life to God—including my music. For the first time, I was open to the witness of young people who had been freed from the deception of rock music, and I was challenged by their purity.

"I humbled myself and asked God to show me the truth of His ways in music. The Lord has clearly and powerfully borne witness in my spirit, and I thank God for the freedom and victory He continues to give me."

Ruthie Fritsch, Oregon

HOW WE REGAINED "GROUND"

The first steps to conquering the addiction of rock music involved recognizing the bitterness, greed, or immorality that gave "ground" to Satan and then through the blood of Christ asking God to regain that which we surrendered.

Matthew

☐ "When I went back to my parents and confessed that I had been disobedient to them, they were surprised. They had no idea that I had rejected their authority with the things I did after listening to rock music. Clearing my conscience in this way was the first step in gaining freedom in my life. I claimed the blood of Christ and asked Him to regain the 'ground' I had given to Satan.

"I also recalled a three-month period when I had worked on a farm and the owners played the radio with 'easy-listening music' which contained the rock beat. I had never realized how many songs I had unknowingly memorized as they were played regularly on the radio. It actually took me years to go back and specifically confess each song that was in my mind. Satan would often bring these songs to my mind to open me to temptation.

"It was like taking garbage out of my mind, bag by bag. By confessing each song and asking God to regain the 'ground,' I was able to rid my soul of this music. The result was a whole new love for the Lord and a deeper relationship of love and respect toward my parents."

Angela

☐ "When I walk into a store or any other place that is playing rock music familiar to my past, I immediately feel spiritual warfare. However, I discovered a method that is very effective in overcoming this music.

"When I hear a rock song, I think of a hymn that contains a spiritual truth that combats the lies in the rock song. I sing that hymn to myself, or even out loud. For example:

Words of Rock Song	_Hymn_
"I can't get no satisfaction."	"Hallelujah! I have found Him, Whom my soul so long has craved!
	Jesus satisfies my longings;
Spiritual Truth	Thro' His blood I now am saved."
Only Jesus can truly satisfy.	

("Satisfied," by Clara T. Williams)

Words of Rock Song	*Hymn*
"I could never live without your love."	"O Love that will not let me go, I rest my weary soul in Thee; I give Thee back the life I owe, That in Thine ocean depths its flow May richer, fuller be."

Spiritual Truth

I should look to Jesus for acceptance. He has already accepted me. *"Greater love hath no man than this that a man lay down his life for his friends."*[25]

("O Love That Will Not Let Me Go," by George Matheson)

"I have found that the spirit of the good music effectively drives away the spirit of the bad music and brings real freedom."

Melissa

☐ "Five years after I stopped listening to Christian and secular rock music, I was by myself one morning, and the words of a wicked song flooded my mind. I was shocked, because normally at that time I would be singing to the Lord.

"The Lord reminded me of my recent prayer that He reveal any area of my soul that was not fully under His control. I realized that even though I neither liked the song nor the singer, I had compromised by not standing up for what was right—thereby passively yielding my members to Satan.

"I immediately asked God to take back His ownership of this part of my mind and cleanse it of this terrible song. At that moment I felt a freedom and a great joy in serving a God Who can break any bondage, no matter how large or small."

Kathy

☐ "When I learned about the dangers of rock music, I tried to avoid it. However, it seemed that this music was everywhere. Hearing it would bring back doubts about God and previous decisions that I knew were right. It gave me feelings of independence.

"All my creative energy was expended in memorizing songs. I didn't have time to pray, because my free time was spent listening to rock music. The bitterness I had toward my mother and stepfather gave much 'ground' to Satan to build many strongholds. I heard the material about how to ask God to take back 'ground,' and I cleared up the bitterness toward my mother and my stepfather. Then I asked God to take back the 'ground' I had given to Satan. Immediately I sensed a quietness in my spirit.

"Every time I heard an old rock song, it was as though I needed a Godly song to counter and replace it, so I began to memorize hymns. This was very effective, and it caused me to appreciate the instruction in Ephesians 5:19 of using Psalms, hymns, and spiritual songs in spiritual warfare."

David

☐ "The first step I took to regain the 'ground' I had given Satan was to confess that I had sinned by my bitterness and rebellion to my parents. I also acknowledged that Satan had control of my life in the area of rock music.

"Then I got rid of all my rock music. That was the easy part. The hard part was getting the music out of me. I had to be careful wherever I went, because if rock music was playing, I would find myself having feelings of rebellion, independence, and wanting to run away. Now I know that those feelings can be traced to strongholds of wrong ideas that need to be torn down by God's truth. Continuous victory for me is possible only as I realize that I am always vulnerable."

Nick

☐ "I did not realize how strongly rock music appealed to my lower nature until I took Scriptural steps to conquer moral impurity. I confessed my failures to the Lord and my father, asked forgiveness of those I offended, and became accountable to my authorities for daily victory.

"God cleansed me, and I became more sensitive and receptive to His grace. I began to meditate on Scripture and to yield each area of my life to God according to Romans 6 and 8, which I had memorized. The more I grew in the Lord, the less "Christian rock" appealed to me. It did not feed my spirit as I once thought it did, and I naturally exchanged it for Godly music that *did* strengthen my spirit.

"Now when I hear rock music in a store or public place, it has little or no influence upon me. If, however, I hear a song from my past, it can become a temptation to give place to the former attitudes of sensuality. To conquer these old songs, I acknowledge the 'ground' that was given, claim the blood of Christ, and ask God to take back the 'ground' for His glory."

How To Cast Down
STRONGHOLDS
OF ROCK MUSIC

Once God has regained surrendered "ground" in the soul, it is then possible to conquer through Him by pulling down *strongholds*. A *stronghold* is a false idea or unscriptural presupposition from which we make wrong decisions. We have found the following six steps very valuable in this process.

"Casting down imaginations, and every high thing that exalteth itself against the knowledge of God, and bringing into captivity every thought to the obedience of Christ" (II Corinthians 10:4–5).

SIX STEPS* TO CAST DOWN

1 Learn God's Law.	**2** See God's Examples.	**3** Apply God's Law.
"The *Law* of the Lord [Torah] **is perfect** [complete; upright], **converting the soul.**"[26]	"**The** *testimony* [witness] **of the Lord is sure** [faithful; firm; certain], **making wise the simple.**"[29]	"**The** *statutes* [mandates of universal morality] **of the Lord are right, rejoicing the heart.**"[33]

The *Law* can refer to the five books of Moses (the Pentateuch). It can also refer to the Ten Commandments (the Decalogue), or the whole Old Testament (the "Law and the Prophets").

The Law is our "schoolmaster" (pedagogue), to bring us to Christ. In New Testament Rome, a *schoolmaster* was a trusted slave who had the responsibility of bringing a child of nobility to the master teacher.

Jesus is our Master Teacher. His Law of Love is a perfect interpretation and application of the Old Testament Law. He taught that all the Law is built upon two great commandments: *". . . Thou shalt love the Lord thy God with all thy heart, and with all thy soul, and with all thy mind and with all thy strength: this is the first commandment.*

"The second is . . . Thou shalt love thy neighbour as thyself. . . ."[27]

It is through the Law that we understand sin.[28]

The *testimonies* of the Lord are His biographies and examples. They are written for us today.[30]

Every situation that we will ever face in life has its parallel in the Bible.

The problems we face are the same type of problems that Abraham, Moses, David, Daniel, Esther, Ruth, and others faced during their lifetimes.

The customs of their times may have changed, but their underlying pressures and decisions are the same, because they are common to human nature. *"There hath no temptation taken you but such as is common to man. . . ."*[31]

It is very important that we find the testimony that is precisely parallel to our situation. The Holy Spirit will help us do this if we ask God for wisdom and apply ourselves to the study of God's Word. *"Study to show thyself approved unto God, a workman that needeth not to be ashamed, rightly dividing the word of truth."*[32]

The *statutes* are the precise applications of the Law to practical situations. They are the concepts of Scripture that "take us by the hand" and lead us to Godly living.

They reveal the true intent of the Law in terms that are understandable.

When David's men came back from a victory in battle, they declared that those who did not fight should not share in the spoil, but David declared that those who "stay by the stuff" are to share equally with those who go out to battle.[34] This became a statute in Israel forever.[35]

Paul illustrated how principles from God's Law apply to life when he instructed churches to give a proper wage to pastors: *"For the Scripture saith, Thou shalt not muzzle the ox that treadeth out the corn. . . ."*[36] Paul pointed out that this Old Testament Law was not written primarily for the ox, but rather for our benefit.[37]

Based on the sequence of Psalm 19:7–10

STRONGHOLDS

4 Make Wise Decisions.	**5** Follow Disciplines.	**6** Report the Results.
"The *commandment* of the Lord is pure [clean, clear], **enlightening the eyes.**"[38]	"The *fear* of the Lord is clean [morally pure], enduring forever." [43]	"The *judgments* of the Lord are true and righteous altogether."[47]

The *commandment* of the Lord is summarized in two points: loving the Lord, and loving others.[39]

Commandments can be given to us either by God or by His ordained authorities, such as government leaders, parents, or church officials.

In Proverbs we are instructed, ". . . *Keep thy father's commandment, and forsake not the law of thy mother. . . . For the commandment is a lamp; and the law is light. . . .*"[40]

When we make a decision to obey a commandment and make our commitment known to God, a brightness occurs in our eyes that is a reflection of the purity of our souls. This light is the most powerful witness of a believer and is what God intends for us to have in order to reveal truth in the world.

"*The light of the body is the eye. . . .*"[41] We are to "*let [our] light so shine that [others will] see [our] good works, and glorify [our] Father which is in heaven.*"[42]

Once we make decisions to apply the Law of the Lord to our lives, it is important that we establish Scriptural disciplines into our daily lives.

Each discipline has a promise of reward attached to it, but God alone knows whether we are carrying it out with the right motives. Our motive should be the fear of the Lord.

The fear of the Lord is the constant awareness that God is watching and evaluating every word, thought, action, and attitude, and that He will reward us accordingly.

God promises that if we fast, pray, or give secretly, He will reward us openly.[44] If we memorize and meditate on Scripture, we will grow spiritually, and whatever we do will be successful.[45]

These disciplines are excellent ways for us to humble ourselves, and "*by humility and the fear of the Lord are riches, and honour, and life.*"[46]

The *judgments* of God are the formal decrees or pronouncements that are given about the actions of people. These judgments teach others about God's Law and cause others to respect the Word of God and to desire to follow His ways.

When Solomon applied the Law of God to the challenging situation of two harlots arguing over a surviving baby, the news of his wise judgment spread through the kingdom and other nations, causing the fear of the Lord to fall upon his people and bringing him international respect.[48]

The more diligent we are in following the first five steps in tearing down strongholds, the more equipped we will be to encourage others by the results in our lives.

The things we learn become the basis for counsel that we can give to others so they, too, can tear down strongholds.

CASTING DOWN THE FALSE IDEA THAT
"MUSIC IS AMORAL"

1 God's Law	2 God's Examples	3 God's Concepts
•Creating an amoral class for music violates the First Commandment, because it robs God of His jurisdiction over music and puts music under *our* authority. •It denies God's omniscience, because He sees all things and evaluates all things as *only* evil or good.[49] •It disregards the pagan origin of rock music.	•The high places of Israel were viewed as amoral. They could be used to worship God or Baal, but God condemned them and wanted them destroyed. •God's creation does not allow for amoral things. He created everything good. Man corrupted it with evil. •Even animals were classified as clean and unclean.	•God equates friendship with the world as spiritual adultery. Those who love the world thereby become the enemies of God. The greatest evidence of admiration is imitation. •Fellowship with things that are offered to the idols of the world unites us with the demons that are connected with those idols.

1 How God's Law Pulls Down the False Idea That Music Is Amoral

At the heart of Satan's deception about rock music is the false presupposition that music is amoral. To say that music is amoral is to state that it is neither good nor evil.

Scripture states that *"the eyes of the Lord are in <u>every place</u>, beholding the evil and the good."*[50] If His eyes are in every place, and all He sees is evil or good, where is the place for amoral things? To say such a thing is to deny God of His omniscience.

God's Law is very clear that He will judge every deed and every word by whether it is good or evil. *"For we must all appear before the judgment seat of Christ; that every one may receive the things done in his body, according to that he hath done, whether it be good or bad."*[51] God makes no provision for "amoral" things.

A further statement of Scripture is that *". . . God shall bring every work into judgment, with every secret thing, whether it be good, or whether it be evil."*[52] Can you imagine a rock musician or a rock addict standing before the judgment seat of Christ and saying, "You can't judge my music; it's amoral!"

2 How the Testimonies of Scripture Refute the Deception of "Amoral Music"

High Places: The high places of Israel were altars that could be used to worship God or Baal. They were usually spared from destruction during spiritual reforms because the people looked upon them as "amoral," but God looked at them as citadels of deception and places of national compromise and backsliding.[53]

Creation: When God finished Creation, Scripture affirms: *"And God saw every thing that he had made, and, behold, it was very good. . . ."*[54] By His own testimony, God created no classification of "amoral things."

Classification of Animals: Similarly, God categorized animals as either *clean* or *unclean*. Even clean animals that were offered to idols became unclean to New Testament believers by the verdict of the Holy Spirit and the Church Council.[55]

Cleansing for Service: When God established the office of the Priest, He required that the Priests be clean before entering into any service, including music. Thus, even those who were sanctified for ministry could be judged as unfit and their music deemed unacceptable.

3 How the Concepts of the Bible Expose the Error of "Amoral Music"

• The Concept of Spiritual Adultery

The Seventh Commandment is, *"Thou shalt not commit adultery."*[56] God applies this command to the concept of loving the world: *"Ye adulterers and adulteresses, know ye not that the friendship of the world is enmity with God? whosoever therefore will be a friend of the world is the enemy of God."*[57]

There is no doubt that rock music is of the world, and we demonstrate our love for the world by copying it, because the greatest evidence of admiration is imitation.

• The Concept of Fellowship With Devils

In I Corinthians 10:15–21, the Apostle Paul makes an amazing analogy between fellowship with Christ which comes at the Communion table and fellowship with demons which comes by association with that which is offered to idols. (Numbers and definitions below from *Strong's Concordance*.)

#2842

#2842

#3348

#2844

15 I speak as to wise men; judge ye what I say.

16 The cup of blessing which we bless, is it not the communion of the blood of Christ? The bread which we break, is it not the communion of the body of Christ?

17 For we being many are one bread, and one body: for we are all partakers of that one bread.

18 Behold Israel after the flesh: are not they which eat of the sacrifices partakers of the altar?

19 What say I then? that the idol is any thing or that which is offered in sacrifice to idols is any thing?

20 But I say, that the things which the Gentiles sacrifice, they sacrifice to devils, and not to God: and I would not that ye should have fellowship with devils.   #2844

21 Ye cannot drink the cup of the Lord, and the cup of devils: ye cannot be partakers of the Lord's table, and of the table of devils.   #3348

Definitions of Words:

#2842 κοινωνία **koinonia,** *koy-noe-NEE-uh; from 2844; partnership,* i.e. (lit.) *participation, or (social) intercourse,* or (pecuniary) *benefaction:*—(to) communicate (-ation), communion, (contri-) distribution, fellowship.

#2844 κοινωνός **koinonos,** *koy-noe-NAWSS; from 2839; a sharer,* i.e., *associate:*— companion, fellowship, partaker, partner.

#3348 μετέχω **metecho,** *meh-TECK-oh; from 3326 [meta] and 2192 [echo]; to share or participate;* by impl. *belong to, eat (or drink):*— be partaker, pertain, take part, use.

Meta is the root word of *metecho.* The Greek use of the word *meta* suggests an "abstract relationship." It is used in such words as *metaphysics,* which refers to that which is "beyond the physical; supernatural; transcendental; subtle; occult."

Why did Paul use the word *meta* to indicate "fellowship"?

The word *meta* describes a relationship. It denotes accompaniment, participation, or proximity. Used in this context, it establishes the fact that participation in an activity, whether at the Communion table or with things offered to Satan, creates a spiritual union.

Scripture states that participating in Communion unites us spiritually (*meta*) with the body and blood of the Lord. Likewise, participating in evil (ungodly activities) unites us spiritually (*meta*) with demons.

The Voodoo Origin of Rock 'n' Roll

Music researchers have presented compelling evidence that rock music has its origin in voodoo worship. The following paragraphs are excerpts from a well-documented research paper on this subject.[58]

"The so-called pagan religions share the conviction that religious worship is a *bodily* celebration. A dance of the entire community."

"The **metaphysical** goal of the African way is to *experience* the intense meeting of the human world and the spirit world. Spurred by the holy drums, deep in the meditation of the dance, one is literally entered by a god or a goddess. Goddesses may enter men, and gods may enter women.... The body literally becomes the crossroads, human and divine are united within it— and it can happen to anyone."

"In Abomey, Africa, these deities that speak through humans are called *vodun*. The word means 'mysteries.' From their *vodun* comes our *Voodoo*, and it is to Voodoo that we must look for the roots of our music. . . ."[59]

"Voodoo is not so much Africa in the New World as it is Africa meeting the New World, absorbing it and being absorbed by it, and reforming the ancient **metaphysics** according to what it now had to face. . . ."[60]

"Protestantism and Voodoo are always at odds. A Haitian saying goes, 'If you want the *loa* [a voodoo god] to leave you alone—become a Protestant [a believer].'"[61]

In explaining the hold that rock music has in evangelical churches and the moral breakdown that is also occurring in these churches, this researcher observes:

"[A church that plays rock 'n' roll is a] church sending out two contradictory signals at the same time, one to the body and one to the mind."

"A doctrine that denies the body [lower nature] preached by a practice that excites the body would eventually drive the body into fulfilling itself elsewhere. Above all denials, the worshiper would long for the body/mind unity felt when the church was 'rocking.' In those churches the African **metaphysic** and the Western **metaphysic** would blend, clash, feed, and battle each other in each and every soul."[62]

"Within thirty years, its impact [American rock 'n' roll] would make an American tune distinguishable from a European tune, no matter how straitlaced the music. It would be a music in all its forms that would reject Puritan America even at its mildest; it would have a beat, and in that beat would be everything that denied the split between the mind [spirit] and the body [lower nature]."[63]

"But we are interested here in how the **metaphysics** lived on in the music, not the practices [of voodoo], now, by what evidence there is, mostly degenerated from transcendence to sorcery. These Voodoo nuances linger as a kind of coda to the direct influences of the indigenous African religion or American culture. From here, the African **metaphysics** will be felt all in the music, all in the body, its direct lineage to Africa a thing of the past."[64]

"Elvis Presley was the first product of African **metaphysics** in America which the official culture could not ignore."

"It is important to recognize that when whites started playing rock 'n' roll, the whole aesthetic of Western performance changed. . . . Spurred by a god within him, the devotee . . . throws himself into a series of improvisations [bodily gestures]. . . . The audience is not taken in: it is to the *loa* [Voodoo god] and not the loa's servant [performer] that their admiration goes out."[65]

"The Voodoo rite of possession by the god *became the standard of American performance in rock 'n' roll.* Elvis Presley, Little Richard, Jerry Lee Lewis, James Brown, Janis Joplin, Tina Turner, Jim Morrison, Johnny Rotten, Prince—they let themselves be possessed not by any god they could name but by the spirit they felt in the music. Their behavior in this possession was something Western society had never before tolerated. And the way a possessed devotee in a Voodoo ceremony often will transmit his state of possession to someone else is by merely touching the hand; Western performers transmitted their possession through their voice and their dance to their audience, even through their records."[66]

"Rock 'n' roll . . . does preserve qualities of that African **metaphysic** intact so strongly that it unconsciously generates the same dances, acts as a major antidote to the mind/body split, and uses a derivative of Voodoo's technique of possession as a source for performers and audience alike, of tremendous personal energy."[67]

"Music can be understood by the body instantly—it carries so much history within it that we don't need history to understand it."[68]

"From the first, the music has felt like an attack on the institutions [marriage, the family, the church, the government, etc.]—actual and conceptual—that it was, in fact, attacking."

"'If I told you what our music is really about, we'd probably all get arrested,' Bob Dylan told an interviewer in 1965."[69]

"It is a music that won't stop, and it won't leave us alone. It speaks through the body and invokes the spirit."[70]

4 How Obeying God's Commands Pulls Down the Stronghold of "Amoral Music"

Regaining "Ground": Because Christ died for our sins on the cross, Satan has no authority in our lives, except the "ground" we give him in our souls.[71] By confessing specific sins of bitterness, greed, or immorality, and claiming the blood of Christ, we overcome Satan.[72] Then, as we verbally ask God to take back the "ground" we surrendered to Satan, God gives an "eviction notice" to Satan, and he must flee.[73]

> *"Heavenly Father, I confess the sin of _____. I now claim the blood of the Lord Jesus Christ as full payment for my sin, and I ask you to take back the 'ground' that I surrendered to Satan by this sin. Thank you for hearing this prayer and restoring this area of my soul. Amen."*

Pull Down the Stronghold: It is now important to verbally reject Satan's deception that music is amoral and to affirm God's truth that all things are either good or evil. By these affirmations, we tear down the stronghold of Satan and establish truth. Jesus rejected Satan's false ideas by quoting Scripture. We can do the same. Here is a suggested prayer:

> *"Heavenly Father, I reject the false idea that music is amoral, and I affirm the truth that your eyes are in every place beholding the evil and the good. Amen."*

Remove Evil Music: God commands us to *". . . make [no] provision for the flesh, to fulfil the lusts thereof."*[74] This would mean destroying rock music or any other items that you know are giving Satan an opportunity to build his false ideas in your soul. If having a radio in your room is a temptation to sin, it would be wise to put the radio somewhere else, where it is less of a temptation to you.

Replace Rock: One of the results of being filled with God's Spirit is to make melody in our hearts for the ears of the Lord. If we take wrong music *out* of our lives, we must replace it with the *right* kind of music.[75]

5 How Biblical Disciplines Reinforce the Truth About "Amoral Music"

Memorize Truth: The most effective way to pull down "strongholds of error" and raise up "towers of truth" is to memorize key passages of Scripture and meditate on them day and night. Following are some verses with which you can begin and which speak directly to the deception of "amoral music":

> *"And God saw every thing that he had made, and, behold, it was very good . . . "* (Genesis 1:31).

> *"The eyes of the Lord are in every place, beholding the evil and the good"* (Proverbs 15:3).

> *"For we must all appear before the judgment seat of Christ; that every one may receive the things done in his body, according to that he hath done, whether it be good or bad"* (II Corinthians 5:10).

> *". . . God shall bring every work into judgment with every secret thing, whether it be good, or whether it be evil"* (Ecclesiastes 12:13).

Study God's Testimonies: We are to study God's Word in order to accurately apply it and thereby show ourselves approved unto God.[76] In an exhaustive concordance, look up all the references to "high places," and make a study of these altars of worship. Notice how they parallel the concept of "amoral music," and observe the moral destruction they brought to God's people.

Fast: Stop listening to all contemporary music for at least a month. After this "music fast," discern if any of your music contains even a faint rock beat. God promises that if we fast secretly, He will reward us openly.[77] (See page 95 for a description of the rock beat.)

Pray: When the words or the beat of a rock song come back to your mind, use them as a signal to regain more "ground" and to tear down more strongholds. Every rock song has its own false messages, imaginations, and proud ideas which must be pulled down with God's truth.

6 *How a Report of Freedom Delivers Others From "Amoral Music"*

Because the idea that music is amoral is the cornerstone of Satan's deception on rock music, you can be confident that he will vigorously oppose anyone who challenges this stronghold.

After you have found freedom from this deception, it would be important to explain to others how you first identified areas of bitterness, greed, or immorality that allowed Satan to gain "ground" in your soul. Explain how you confessed these root sins, claimed the blood of Christ, and asked God to take back the "ground" that was given to Satan.

Then point out that you were able to recognize and tear down the false idea of "amoral music" only after you regained the "ground" and searched out the Scriptures that refuted this idea.

It is important to remember the warnings of Scripture not to argue about the false ideas of strongholds.[78] Instead, focus on the tormentors someone may be experiencing in his life, such as fear, depression, anger, and lust, and show him how to trace these tormentors to surrendered "ground."

Summary of Conquering Strongholds

4 *Wise Decisions*	5 *Disciplines*	6 *Results*
• Reject the deception of "amoral music" as a violation of Scriptural truth. • Quote the truth of God's Word regarding all things being good or evil. • Purpose to cleanse your home and heart of all music that is displeasing to God or your parents. • Decide to put a new song in your heart of true praise to God.	• Memorize verses that confirm that all things are good or evil. • Study the testimonies of strongholds. • Cleanse your home of all evil music. • Go on a "music fast" of all contemporary music for at least one month. • Learn the great hymns of faith, and make melody in your heart to the Lord.	• Write out your testimony of how you regained "ground" given to Satan and how that freed you to tear down strongholds of false ideas, such as "music is amoral." • Don't argue over strongholds, but help the other person identify tormentors, and explain how he can remove them by confessing root sins.

A Confirming Witness Linking Rock Music To Satan Worship

"When I was about seven, I became involved in a Satanic coven. We had been having severe family problems, and my mother met a policeman who was involved in a church youth group. She thought he would be a good role model for me and that the church would provide a good place for me to grow as a young person.

"I believe the church was legitimate, but the youth group was actually an open door for Satanism. It used the church as a front to get young people involved in Satanic cults. Since this was the first church and youth group I had ever attended, it took a while before I realized that the kinds of things we were doing in the group weren't the kinds of things that other people probably did in their churches.

"I grew up with a 'Star Wars' mentality. I loved Star Wars and the whole concept of the dark side and the forces of darkness. Those things were very important to me. I also enjoyed other science fiction movies.

"When I was eight and a half, I was involved in my first ritual sacrifice. This was the first I remember when I wasn't under the control of either alcohol or drugs. Often, when we recruited young people to our meetings, we gave them alcohol or drugs so they would have a hard time remembering what had taken place.

"I was involved quite heavily in Satanic worship for seven years in three different covens because we moved. When we moved, a group in the new area involved me in the local coven. When I was fifteen, we moved again. I decided not to get involved with any other Satanic coven, but I purposed to become a self-styled Satanist and practice my worship of Satan by myself. This lasted for two and a half years.

"Satanic worship services are designed to put the worshipers into a mood where spirits can be called to manifest themselves during the service. They always use live music, and the music always has a beat.

"They start with a drummer. The rest of the instruments are geared to the drumming. These people practiced many, many hours for every service we had. **It was rock music with a rock beat.** We were told that the reason they used the rock beat was because it's the same beat as your heart.

"Subconsciously, while you listened to the music, it would open you up. People weren't aware that they were opening up to spirits, because they were concentrating on the music. The music is a great part of the service because it opens you up to spirits without your being aware of it. This music prepared everyone to open themselves up to the forces of darkness.

"As those forces respond to that invitation, people become inhabited by demons. There is no way to carry out the things done in those services without inviting spirits into your life to empower you to do them. During those services, I saw atrocities and vile acts. People turned against their friends with savagery, even becoming cannibalistic.

"I am now in my twenties. I am asking God to bring healing from my involvement in Satanism and the horrors of those years of my life. **Whenever I hear rock music, whether it's supposedly Christian or not, my reaction is extreme. I can't handle the music. I don't care what the words say. As soon as I hear the beat, it takes me back to those services where we called the enemy to empower us to do great evil. I am grieved about 'Christian rock' music. I can't believe Christians accept these things.**

"Whenever I attend a church service where 'Christian rock' is played, I have to leave. I can't stay. It triggers so many memories, feelings, and emotions that I can't control my thoughts, whether the words are Christian or not.

"I can't expose myself in any way to that kind of beat in music. As much as I can, I avoid any place where rock music is played. With my background, it's very difficult for me to understand why any Christian would want to put Christian words to that kind of music.

"I have to believe they are sincere, but I do not believe they really understand what they're opening themselves up to and the invitation they are giving the enemy to their lives. When I hear rock music in church, to me it's like taking a Ouija board to church and saying, 'We're going to play this and not summon the powers of darkness. We're going to play this and try to get a message from God.' It just doesn't fit.

"I attended one church service where a young man ran out of the room making noises as they started playing rock music. When I ran after him, I found him down the hall on his knees crying. He looked at me and said, 'You were in a coven, too, weren't you?' I said that I had been, and he said, 'I can't stand the thoughts that are coming into my mind because of that music. Why are they using it in this church? I thought it would be different here.'

"Even ten or twenty years from now, I believe if I'm in some type of Christian service where they use 'Christian rock,' I will still struggle with the horrible thoughts triggered in my mind by the music used in the Satanic covens. I think hearing it, even in a church, will always trigger terrible thoughts for me.

"One of the many things they trained us for in the coven was understanding music. A number of us were taken to a fellow who had a lot of involvement in a large music industry. He explained to us that wherever we went in the world, we would hear that kind of music, and there would be people worshiping Satan. He played sections of music from different countries, beginning with Ireland, throughout Europe, and into Africa. It was part of our training to understand that all over the world, people are able to call spirits through music. Even if we left the United States, it would follow us. The music was used to prove it to us.

"I would ask those of you who read this to pray for me. I have been out of Satanism for several years now and just recently went through the steps to freedom with Rev. Logan. God has helped me to put a lot of this behind me. I still have a lot to work through; I have many terrible memories which must be dealt with in a Biblical way so I can continue to experience the freedom that God has begun in my life."

The testimony of a twenty-year-old man, verified by Dr. Jim Logan

International Center for Biblical Counseling
1551 Indian Hills Drive, Suite 200
Sioux City, IA 51104

CASTING DOWN THE FALSE IDEA THAT
"THE WORDS MAKE IT RIGHT"

1 God's Law	2 God's Examples	3 God's Concepts
• The Ninth Commandment is, *"Thou shalt not bear false witness. . . ."* Rock music gives a contradictory message, thus making it false. • The law of the clean and unclean would prohibit the use of Godly words in ungodly music. • God commands us to have no fellowship with the unfruitful works of darkness, but rather to reprove them. • God's people were forbidden to make any alliance with the ungodly. • The Fifth Commandment would prohibit listening to such music if parents are against it.	• A demon used the right words when giving testimony of Jesus: *"I know thee who thou art, the Holy One of God,"* but Jesus rebuked and silenced the demon. • The clairvoyant girl gave the right testimony about Paul and Silas: *"These men are the servants of the most high God, which show unto us the way of salvation,"* but Paul was grieved and rebuked the spirit in her. • Balaam was true to the message God gave him, but he was associated with God's enemies and experienced God's judgment.	• Light cannot have fellowship with darkness, neither the temple of God with the temple of the devil. • Mixing hot and cold produces that which is lukewarm. The same is true of mixing Godly and ungodly music: it is nauseating to God. • Christians are not to link up with the world to do God's work. • Music during warfare must be clear. *". . . If the trumpet give an uncertain sound, who shall prepare himself [for] battle?"* • Sheep must learn to flee the voice of the stranger.

1 How God's Law Rejects the Lie That "The Words Make It Right"

Eagerness to justify rock music by any means is a further symptom of addiction to it, and to argue that rock music is made right by Christian words is evidence of a major stronghold of Satan. The devil used Biblical words when he tempted Jesus in the wilderness, but those words did not make the temptation right.[79] Peter used "Christian words" when he talked to Jesus about the cross, but Jesus recognized them as words from Satan and rebuked Satan.[80]

When we consider that God created all languages[81] but that man can corrupt them,[82] and when we consider that Jesus spoke no words except those that the Heavenly Father gave Him,[83] one important fact comes into focus:

The words we speak can come from God; they can also come from Satan. We are commanded to discern the source of our words before we speak them and the source of others' words after they are spoken.

Jesus demonstrated this with Peter, and in the same way we must demonstrate it with the words of all music. When Peter said to Jesus, "*. . . Thou art the Christ, the Son of the living God,*" Jesus assured him that those words were given to him from "*. . . my Father which is in heaven.*"

Shortly after this, Jesus explained to the disciples that He would be killed and raised from the dead. Peter said, "*. . . Be it far from thee, Lord: this shall not be unto thee.*" These words were intended to be a support to Jesus, but Jesus replied, "*. . . Get thee behind me, Satan: thou art an offence unto me: for thou savourest not the things that be of God, but those that be of men.*"[84]

The Apostle Paul urged his hearers to investigate all of his words to see whether they were of God.[85] To justify rock music simply because it has some spiritual words to it is to deny all these important factors as well as the following commands.

The Law Against a False Witness:

The Ninth Commandment prohibits any person from bearing false witness.[86] Rock music has a message all its own. It is a message of rebellion against authority and morality. Its message is totally contrary to the Holiness of God and is recognized universally to be so.

To put Christian words to this kind of message is contradictory. One message fights against the other. To give both messages together is to be hypocritical and false. "*A false witness shall not be unpunished. . . .*"[87]

The Law of the Clean and Unclean:

God commanded the Priests to teach the difference "*. . . between the holy and profane . . . between the unclean and the clean*"[88] To combine holy words with profane music is contrary to

Scripture. This distinction between clean and unclean, holy and profane, is further emphasized in the New Testament.

Christians are instructed to be separated from the practices of the world, *". . . What agreement hath the temple of God with idols? for ye are the temple of the living God; as God hath said, I will dwell in them, and walk in them; and I will be their God, and they shall be my people. Wherefore come out from among them, and be ye separate, saith the Lord, and touch not the unclean thing; and I will receive you."*[89]

The Law Against Fellowship With Darkness:

Rock music is the music and the message of darkness. As believers we are commanded to *". . . have no fellowship with the unfruitful works of darkness, but rather reprove them,"*[90] because God is Light, and in Him is no darkness at all. If we use rock music with Christian words, we create a combination of light and darkness which is still a shade of darkness. We are thus violating the nature of God and failing to be the light of the world.

The Law Against Unholy Alliances:

God's people are given strict instructions not to make alliances with the ungodly. Any attempts to unite the Christian world and the secular world through rock music is a clear violation of God's command, *". . . Ye shall make no league with the inhabitants of the land; ye shall throw down their altars. . . ."*[91]

God's judgment repeatedly fell upon His people because of their tendency to combine worship of Him with the sensual worship of heathen gods. When Israel *". . . did not destroy the nations, concerning whom the Lord commanded them: But were mingled among the heathen, and learned their works, and they served their idols: which were a snare unto them. ... Therefore was the wrath of the Lord kindled against his people, insomuch that he abhorred his own inheritance. And he gave them into the hand of the heathen; and they that hated them ruled over them."*[92]

The Command to Honor Parents:

The Fifth Commandment is, *"Honour thy father and thy mother: that thy days may be long upon the land which the Lord thy God giveth thee."*[93] The importance of this command is emphasized in the New Testament. *"Honour thy father and mother; which is the first com-*

mandment with promise; That it may be well with thee, and thou mayest live long on the earth."[94] Christian leaders who allow, encourage, or promote "Christian rock" music are very aware of the vehement objections of many parents.

Aside from any merits of the music, such leaders are obligated by Scripture to teach sons and daughters to obey their parents in this matter. To do otherwise would be to contribute to the alienation and any resulting delinquency of minors.

They would also be guilty of defying the work of God to ". . . turn the heart of the fathers to the children, and the heart of the children to their fathers, lest I come and smite the earth with a curse."[95]

2 How God's Testimonies Show the Lie of "The Words Make It Right"

If sound Christian words were acceptable to God by whatever means they were given, then Jesus would not have silenced the demons, and Paul would never have silenced the clairvoyant girl. They each gave clear witness to the truth, but God has ordained that those who speak the truth must live it.

The Testimony of Jesus:

The right words were given by a man in the synagogue during the time of Jesus. When others wondered who Jesus was, this man loudly proclaimed, ". . . I know thee who thou art, the Holy One of God." Rather than being pleased with this truthful statement, Jesus recognized that its source was an unclean spirit. ". . . Jesus rebuked him, saying, Hold thy peace, and come out of him. And when the unclean spirit had torn him, and cried with a loud voice, he came out of him."[96]

The Testimony of Paul:

When Paul and his companions were walking to the Temple to pray, a girl followed them and called out, ". . . These men are the servants of the most high God, which show unto us the way of salvation." The words sounded good; however, they were spoken from a spirit of divination. Therefore, Paul rebuked the spirit: ". . . I command thee in the name of Jesus Christ to come out of her."[97]

The Testimony of Balaam:

As long as the Israelites were slaves in Egypt, they posed no threat to Balak and his kingdom. However, when Israel was freed, King Balak of Moab tried to hire Balaam to curse Israel so they would not prosper.

Balaam asked God for permission to do this, and God refused to give it. King Balak then sent a more distinguished delegation and offered Balaam more money if he would come and curse God's people.

Once again, Balaam asked God if he could go with them. God gave him the desire of his heart but warned him to speak only the words He gave. Balaam went with the delegation, *"and God's anger was kindled because he went. . . ."*[98]

The king pointed out the people to curse, but instead of cursing them, Balaam blessed them. His words were correct, but because he was associated with God's enemies, Balaam experienced the wrath and judgment of God.

When King Balak could not curse God's people, he invited them to join their sacrificial services. This was the beginning of mixing worship of God with the sensual practices of Baal, and it brought about the destruction of the nation.[99]

There is a striking parallel between the account of Balaam and the history of rock music in the church.

3 *How God's Concepts Reject the False Idea That "The Words Make It Right"*

The music we hear creates pictures in our minds. If we hear march music, we picture an army. If we hear circus music, we picture clowns, animals, and acrobats. When we hear rock music, we picture the performers and the lifestyle they represent.

The observation that a picture is worth a thousand words emphasizes the fact that the images created by the music far outweigh the value of any words that may be added to this kind of music.

The Concept of an Unequal Yoke:

Bob Beasley

God's Law prohibited yoking animals of different types and sizes, such as a donkey and an ox. *"Thou shalt not plow with an ox and an ass together."*[100] Such a combination is not only cruel to the animals but ineffective in accomplishing the task.

In the New Testament, God applies this law in prohibiting believers from trying to work with unbelievers. He explains it as trying to link Christ with the devil. To put Christian words to rock music is to violate the principle of this law. Notice the questions that God asks about an unequal yoke:

". . . What fellowship hath righteousness with unrighteousness? and what communion hath light with darkness? And what [agreement] hath Christ with Belial? or what part hath he that believeth with an infidel? And what agreement hath the temple of God with idols? for ye are the temple of the living God. . . ."[101] What relationship does a Godly message have with voodoo worship?

The Concept of Mixing Hot and Cold:

To combine Christian words with secular rock is like mixing hot and cold. God gives a harsh rebuke to the product that comes from such a mixture: *"I know thy works, that thou art neither cold nor hot: I would thou wert cold or hot. So then because thou art lukewarm, and neither cold nor hot, I will spue thee out of my mouth."*[102]

If a lukewarm Christian is nauseating to God, how much more will God "vomit up" the music that combines Christian words and ungodly music!

The Concept of Aiding the Enemy:

Every believer is in a state of warfare with the enemies of God. *"Be sober, be vigilant; because your adversary the devil, as a roaring lion, walketh about, seeking whom he may devour: Whom resist stedfast in the faith. . . ."*[103]

The enemy is relentless and clever. It would be unthinkable in warfare for soldiers from one camp to join forces with the enemy of the opposite camp. In legal terms, this action is called *treason* and is punishable by death. Uniting Christian words to worldly music is doing in the spiritual world what is considered the most despised crime of a soldier.

One obvious consequence of such an alliance is confusion in the camp. God makes reference to this military concept when He requires a clear and distinct trumpet call: *"For if the trumpet give an uncertain sound, who shall prepare himself to the battle?"*[104]

The Concept of Vulnerability to False Shepherds:

One of the clearest warnings in Scripture is to be alert to the danger of false shepherds. The purpose of these shepherds is in direct opposition to the purpose of Christ. *"Beware of false prophets, which come to you in sheep's clothing, but inwardly they are ravening wolves."*[105]

It is significant that Jesus used sheep as an analogy of believers. Sheep are followers and very vulnerable. They need a shepherd to protect them, and their safety is in following the right shepherd. Their only built-in defense is an instinctive fear of the voice of strangers who would steal from the flock.

If sheep fail to learn this protection, they are vulnerable to destruction. Thus, in speaking of Christ the Good Shepherd, Scripture states, *". . . The sheep follow him: for they know his voice. And a stranger will they not follow, but will flee from him: for they know not the voice of strangers."*[106]

The vile lyrics and music of today's rock performers certainly characterize the kind of strangers from which every believer should flee. Even those who promote "Christian rock" will agree that there are certain types of rock music that are wrong and should be rejected.

However, because the rock beat is addictive and the music sounds just the same as the world's, "Christian rock" music trains believers not only to learn the voice of the stranger, but also to become addicted to it.

If a Christian leader warns believers that there are certain types of evil rock music, but then asks believers to follow him in learning the rock beat with Christian words, how will God evaluate this leader as a shepherd?

4 *How Decisions Pull Down the False Idea That "The Words Make It Right"*

Confessing Sins: The existence of this stronghold would indicate the need to confess several sins. For each sin we must acknowledge that we were wrong and claim the redeeming blood of the Lord Jesus Christ.

- Bearing false witness with a contradictory message
- Failing to distinguish between the holy and the profane
- Having fellowship with the works of darkness
- Making an unholy alliance with Satan and his music
- Disobeying the commandment to honor parents

Regaining Ground: Whenever a sin involves rebellion to God-given authority, "ground" is given to Satan, because *". . . rebellion is as the sin of witchcraft . . ."*[107] and witchcraft is surrendering to the power of Satan. It would be good to pray:

> *"Heavenly Father, I have sinned by violating Your commandments and thereby I have given 'ground' to Satan. I now confess these sins of [name specific sins] and I claim the blood of the Lord Jesus Christ for my cleansing. I ask You to take back the 'ground' I have given Satan in my soul. Thank You for hearing and answering this prayer based on Christ's victory over Satan on the cross. Amen."*

Tearing Down Strongholds: Every rock song that has become a part of your soul carries with it false presuppositions and false ideas. Each song must be destroyed and replaced with Biblical truth.

When you hear a rock song or remember a rock song, reject it as coming from Satan, not from God. Quote Jesus' words to Peter, *"Get thee behind me, Satan: . . . for thou savourest not the things that be of God, but those that be of men."*[108]

Singing a New Song: Each rock song must be replaced by a Godly song. Have melodious songs with Biblical truths memorized so you can instantly use them.

5 How Disciplines Replace the Error of "The Words Make It Right"

In order to tear down the strongholds of false ideas, we must build up fortresses of truth.

Understand the Character of God: The music that fills our hearts and is heard from our lips must be consistent with the character and nature of God. God has revealed Himself to us by the meaning of His names, His attributes, and His actions in the world. List as many of them as you can that directly relate to music, such as the following:

- **The Holy God** – *"Worship God in the beauty of Holiness"*
- **The Creator** – *Who separated light from darkness*
- **The Beginning and the End** – *Orderly compositions*
- **The Judge of All the Earth** – *No compromise with evil*
- **The Shepherd of Our Souls** – *Know only His voice*
- **The Ruler Over Principalities** – *Not co-equal with Satan*
- **The King of Peace** – *Not the confusion of discordant music*
- **The God of Light** – *In Him there is no darkness at all*

Replace Error With Truth: Write down the ideas that are contained in the words and music of rock songs. Then find Scriptures to refute each false idea. Here are some examples:

The Error of Strongholds	The Truth of Scripture
The term *rock 'n' roll* is derived from vulgar, immoral actions.	"Christian *rock*" is saying, "Christian *immorality*"—how absurd! God hates all evil and all whoremongers.[109]
Many phrases mean one thing to a Christian and something different to the world, so they are sung by both. For example, "I will be here for you, somewhere in the night. . . ."	God warns Christians not to be plundered by vain (empty) philosophies, those which leave Christ out.[110] Also, *"If the trumpet give an uncertain sound, who shall prepare himself to the battle?"*[111]

The Error of Strongholds	The Truth of Scripture
Statements from a "Christian rock" song: *"Baby, baby, I'm taken with the notion."*	Our thoughts are not to take *us* captive, rather we are *". . . to [bring] into captivity every thought to the obedience of Christ."*[112]
"Ever since the day you put my heart in motion – baby I realize there's no getting over you."	God commands, *"Keep thy heart with all diligence, for out of it are the issues of life."*[113] *God* is to put our heart in motion—not other people.
"That's what love is for, to help us through it, that's what love is for, nothing else can do it."	Love alone does not "help us through it," but *Christ* alone. *"I can do all things through Christ which strengtheneth me."*[114]

Evaluate the Message of Every Song: Continue this procedure whenever you hear a song. If you need wisdom, ask God for it. He will give it to you as you *"study to show thyself approved unto God, a workman that needeth not to be ashamed, rightly dividing the word of truth."*[115]

Rediscover the Great Hymns of the Faith: There is a wealth of spiritual treasures in the great hymns of the faith. Those who promote "Christian rock" often ridicule the rich heritage of great hymns and try to remove them from churches. Hymns that for decades and even centuries have fulfilled the requirements of Scripture in teaching truth to believers and helping them worship God[116] are now lost to multitudes of youth who have never even heard them.

Much of the richness of our hymn heritage is in knowing about the circumstances that motivated the author to write the hymn. By learning these hymn histories and the Scripture that the hymns are based on, we are able to make greater application of their truths to our lives.

Make Melody in Your Heart: After memorizing at least ten to fifteen hymns, sing them to the Lord throughout the day, and in times of special need, share them with others.

Note: A word of caution regarding hymns is necessary, however. Many newer recordings of hymns are incorporating a rock beat—especially taped accompaniments for vocalists. Discernment is needed here, as well.

6 How Freedom From the Lie That "The Words Make It Right" Gives Wisdom

Annie Dú Breuil (22) has shared her testimony with tens of thousands of people in America, New Zealand, Russia, Australia, Taiwan, and Singapore.

Both of Annie's parents have been in mental hospitals all her life, and her mother tried to commit suicide when Annie was still in the womb. The struggles that she faces each day are opening up rich insight into Scripture.

"The Lord has chosen to place me in a position where I don't have the counsel, comfort, or protection of my parents. Instead, they look to *me* to encourage *them*.

"I began listening to the words of contemporary Christian songs, but they brought back memories from the past and fed my emotions. Very quickly the beat took over. Then I discovered the great hymns of the faith.

"I went through a hymnbook and wrote a personal testimony to each hymn that stood out to me. The words of the hymns are so fulfilling and rich and stay with me when I'm going through a struggle.

"One day I visited my mother, and she talked about committing suicide. On the way home, the words of the hymn *Day by Day* came to me. It was as though the Lord Himself was singing it to me. A tremendous peace filled my heart.

"My parents have been separated in different hospitals since I was born, but there is a new sense of togetherness as I call each one, sing a hymn to them, and ask my father to close in prayer. He hesitates to pray, but his prayers are the most sincere statements I have ever heard.

"I keep my hymnbook with me at all times and find many opportunities to share the hymns with others."

Annie Dú Breuil, Illinois

"ROCK REACHES THE LOST"

1 *God's Law*	2 *God's Examples*	3 *God's Concepts*
• God ordained *preaching* to save the lost, not worldly music. • God ordained music to strengthen believers and to worship Him. • Those who preach the Gospel must fulfill strict requirements. They should be ordained and are not to minister for money.	• God gives numerous examples of saving the lost through preaching, but none through music. • David used melodious music to minister to Saul. • The sons of Sceva were attacked by demons when they ministered, because they were unqualified.	• God's Law is to be used as a schoolmaster to bring us to Christ. • God's grace is the desire and power that He gives to fulfill His righteousness. • Vain philosophies leave out Christ, plunder Christians, and draw away disciples with "perverse" words.

1 *How God's Law Exposes the Confusion of "Rock Reaching the Lost"*

The argument that rock music is leading people to Christ sounds very convincing until this rationalization is analyzed in light of God's Law. God's Law is concerned with the *way* things are done as well as *what* is done. To God, the end does *not* justify the means. In fact, His strict judgment has always come upon those who try to carry out His work in their own way.

What parent will not rejoice when a longed-for baby is born, and who will not rejoice when sinners are born again? But justifying a rock concert because of those who are "reached" is like glorifying a sex orgy because of all the children who will be born.

Think about the difficulty that such children will have as they grow up in a normal world and talk to teenagers who have been freed from rock music. They will tell you about the continual struggle they are having to separate the sensual effects of their past experiences from the spiritual desires they have for the Lord.

God Ordained Preaching to Reach the Lost:

God has ordained that the Gospel be presented through preaching to the conscience of a person, not through a sensual performance to the emotions.[117] The Gospel requires *repentance,* which means turning from our way of life to His way of Holiness and separation from the world.

Using the world's music is not only giving a different message, but a contradictory one. It is saying, "You can come to Christ but still have your old way of life." This is a different Gospel and a strange religion. Paul declared, *". . . Though we, or an angel from heaven, preach any other Gospel unto you than that which we have preached unto you, let him be accursed."*[118]

To attract people to a meeting with rock music and then "slip in the Gospel" is also deceptive. Such a method was rejected by Paul when he said, *"But have renounced the hidden things of dishonesty, not walking in craftiness, nor handling the word of God deceitfully; but by manifestation of the truth commending ourselves to every man's conscience in the sight of God."*[119]

God Ordained Music to Edify and Worship:

God ordained music for two purposes: to edify other believers, and to worship the Lord. *"Speaking to yourselves in psalms and hymns and spiritual songs"* and *"singing and making melody in your heart to the Lord."*[120] The fact is that many Christians have been offended and damaged by "Christian rock" music, but our pleas and objections have been overruled by those who claim that the chief purpose of this music is to reach the lost.

There seems to be no concern about how this music is affecting Christians. The only focus is how it appeals to non-Christians. This justification is to accommodate a personal addiction to the rock beat; however, it still violates the law of love that is given to us by Paul in a parallel illustration of meat that was offered to idols.

"For none of us liveth to himself . . . let us therefore follow after the things which make for peace, and things wherewith one may edify another. For meat [or rock music] *destroy not the work of God: All things indeed are pure; but it is evil for that man who eateth* [or plays rock

music] *with offence. It is good neither to eat flesh, nor to drink wine, nor anything whereby thy brother stumbleth, or is offended, or is made weak.*"[121]

There are those who claim that they have liberty in Christ to play this kind of music. To such a claim God's law again speaks, "*. . . Take heed lest by any means this liberty of yours become a stumblingblock to them that are weak. . . . But when ye sin so against the brethren, and wound their weak conscience, ye sin against Christ.*"[122]

There are thousands of us young people who will affirm that we have been offended and damaged and weakened by "Christian rock" music. We have come to the Lord's table for spiritual nourishment and come away with food poisoning. We have come to church asking for spiritual bread and we have received rock. "*. . . What man is there of you, whom if his son ask bread, will he give him a stone?*"[123]

If a restaurant serves delicious food, but one in every ten customers gets food poisoning, will the health department be impressed with thousands of testimonials from satisfied customers?

If the health department closes down a restaurant when just a few people get food poisoning, how much more should the church close down the rock bands when many of us Christian young people are being spiritually damaged!

We are commanded to do good unto all men, but especially to believers.[124] This command is especially urgent for our day, because we are sacrificing Christians in an attempt to reach non-Christians. The concern that God has for believers is illustrated in his parable about the Shepherd going after even one member of the flock that has gone astray. Our method seems to be, leave the whole flock in order to reach the goats that are not even a part of the flock.[125]

God Ordained Standards for All Who Minister:

Those who minister to Christians in the church are called *ministers*—not performers. They are governed by strict qualifications, including the following: "*. . . Of good behaviour . . . Not greedy of filthy lucre . . . not covetous. . . . Not a novice [newly come to the faith],* *lest being lifted up with pride he fall into the condemnation of the devil."* He must *". . . have a good report of them which are without; lest he fall into reproach and the snare of the devil."*[126]

The ordination committee of a church is charged with the responsibility of investigating the qualifications of those who minister to the flock. Therefore, they are responsible to also investigate any musicians who are teaching those under their spiritual care through the message of the music and lyrics.

2 How God's Examples Reject the Idea That "Rock Reaches the Lost"

The method that God used to begin the early Church was not the attraction of a music team, but preaching that brought conviction and repentance to the hearers.

The Church spread across Asia and around the world through clear, Biblical preaching. Although Paul and Silas did sing hymns in prison and were heard by the captive audience of guards and others, there is no mention of any music ministry used to reach the lost as the Church spread from city to city.[127]

God's Design for Church Growth:

In order for the church to be strong, it must be pure. The purity of believers results in the brightness of their eyes and countenance, and this is the light that will draw people to Christ: *"The light of the body is the eye . . ."* therefore, *"Let your light so shine before men, that they may see your good works, and glorify your father which is in heaven."*[128]

In order for God to protect the purity of the church, He has put a natural hesitation in the heart of unbelievers against joining with believers. After all, how can light have fellowship with darkness? Believers in the early Church were highly esteemed by all the people in the city because of their good works; however, **"no man [dared] join himself to them."** The marvelous results were that *"believers were the more added to the Lord, multitudes, both of men and women."*[129]

Notice that the lost were reached not by believers' compromising their standards to become like them, but by their communicating the power of God that comes through holy living.

Man's Design for Church Growth:

By using "Christian rock" music to reach the lost, the churches of our day are both violating and reversing God's design. Rather than sending Godly Christians into the world from a pure church, the goal is to bring the world into the church in order to "reach them with the Gospel."

In order to break down the God-given barrier for nonbelievers to join believers, the church is compromising its function to appear to be something different than a church. It communicates the image of being a rock concert hall, a gymnasium, or an entertainment center.

Some churches are even advertising that they will not make visitors feel uncomfortable by any preaching that would bring conviction to them. As the world enters the church, the believers lower their standards, and the Godly members are either forced to compromise their convictions, or leave.

David's Ministry to Saul:

When King Saul was overcome with an evil spirit, David was called in to minister to him. It would be unthinkable that David would use rock music with its demonic origins to minister to one who was being tormented by a demon. Instead, he played melodious music on his harp, which the evil spirit could not stand, and thus it fled.[130]

It should be equally unthinkable that Christians would use rock music to try to reach people who are being controlled by the power of Satan.

The Danger of Ministry Without Authority:

There is nothing new about self-appointed ministers of the Gospel. In the days of Paul, seven sons of a man named Sceva took it upon themselves to cast out evil spirits.

The words they used sounded good, *"We adjure you by Jesus whom Paul preacheth. . . ."* When they said this, the evil spirit *". . . answered and said, Jesus I know, and Paul I know; but who are ye? And the man in whom the evil spirit was leaped on them, and overcame them, and prevailed against them, so that they fled out of that house naked and wounded."*

The report of this event became known to all the people in Ephesus, *". . . And fear fell on them all, and the name of the Lord Jesus was magnified."* Then many believers confessed things that they had been doing in secret and burned their occult books in a public bonfire, *"so mightily grew the word of God and prevailed."*[131]

This dramatic account confirms that reaching the lost is not simply a matter of getting their attention and appealing to their emotions, but it is rather a demonstration of God's power and holiness, which brings the fear of God upon all men.

3 How Biblical Concepts Reveal the Fallacy That "Rock Reaches the Lost"

The Concept of the Schoolmaster:

Reaching the lost involves bringing them to the Lord Jesus Christ for salvation. God has established a method by which this is to be done, *"Wherefore the law was our schoolmaster to bring us unto Christ, that we might be justified by faith."*[132]

A schoolmaster was not a teacher but a trusted slave hired by a family of nobility to bring their child to the teacher. The schoolmaster was a strict disciplinarian and would not allow the child under his care to pick up the ways of the world. To use rock music in the place of a schoolmaster would be an inconsistency in God's way of bringing people to Christ.

The Concept of Grace:

The grace of God is not a "license" to reject the Law of God. Rather, it is the desire and the power that God gives to us to carry out His righteousness. Paul emphasized this concept when he said, ". . . I labored more abundantly than they all: yet not I, but the grace of God which was with me."[133]

God gives the desire and the power to every person to do His will; however, that grace can be resisted, "For the grace of God that bringeth salvation hath appeared to all men, Teaching us that, denying ungodliness and worldly lusts, we should live soberly, righteously, and godly, in this present world."[134] God's grace can also be corrupted and perverted.

Those who pervert the grace of God claim that God's grace gives them the freedom to reject the Law of God and to do whatever pleases them. Paul warns about these types of people. "Beloved . . . contend for the faith which was once delivered unto the saints. For there are certain men crept in unawares, who were before of old ordained to this condemnation, ungodly men, turning the grace of our God into lasciviousness. . . ."[135]

Any attempt to combine ungodly, worldly music to teach the things of Christ is corrupting the grace of God. God's grace is necessary for a believer to have in order to grow spiritually, so even if one were brought to Christ through rock music, the music would grieve the Holy Spirit and quench His grace in the life of the believer.[136]

The Concept of Vain Philosophies:

God warns believers not to be plundered by those who promote empty philosophies: "Beware lest any man spoil you through philosophy and vain deceit." This passage goes on to explain what vain philosophies are—anything that leaves Christ out: "After the tradition of men, after the rudiments of the world, and not after Christ."[137]

The whole field of "cross-over" music would fall under this condemnation. At best, this music has double messages, but in order not to offend the world, it leaves out any clear message of the redeeming work of Christ.

We are warned that in the last times shall, ". . . grievous wolves enter in among you, not sparing the flock. Also of your own selves shall men arise, speaking perverse things, to draw away disciples after them."[138]

4 *How Biblical Decisions Enlighten the Eyes to Effectively Reach the Lost*

Brighten Your Eyes: When accurate Biblical decisions are made by a believer, the darkness in the heart is replaced by light, and this light of truth is seen by others in the light of the eyes.

Decide to Reject Error: If you have accepted the false idea that rock music is right because it reaches people for Christ, then in sincere prayer, reject that error because of the following Biblical truths:

- Spiritual children, as with physical children, can be brought into the world by unwholesome methods.
- God ordained preaching, not music, to reach the lost.
- Music is designed to edify believers and worship God.
- All who minister must meet Godly standards.
- God designed the church to be pure.
- God gave unbelievers natural cautions against joining the church.
- Casting out Satan with Satan's music doesn't make sense.
- The Law is God's schoolmaster to bring us to Christ.
- Rock music perverts God's grace and hinders growth.
- Any music that leaves Christ out is vain.

"Heavenly Father, I acknowledge and accept the truths of Your Word as they relate to music, and I hereby reject the false notion that rock music is right because it reaches the lost. I ask You to tear down the stronghold in my soul and replace it with the truth about Your way of bringing people to salvation. Amen."

Correct Error You Have Given to Others: If you have encouraged others to listen to rock music in order to reach them for the Lord or to help them grow in their Christian life, or for some other reason, it would be important to do all you can to inform them of the truth that you have now discovered.

Give them your own personal testimony of how you have recognized the addictive nature of rock music and what effect it has had in your own life. Then explain how you have been able to experience freedom by regaining ground and tearing down the strongholds of error. The contents of this book could be used as a guide to help you accomplish this objective.

Purpose to Use God's Law: Because God has ordained the Law to be a schoolmaster to bring people to Christ, memorize the Ten Commandments and write out a testimony of how you have broken these Commandments. Include also how God has paid the penalty for your violations through the death of Christ and how this knowledge and decision has delivered you from the certain judgment of eternal hell that otherwise awaited you.

5 *How Biblical Disciplines Build a Life Message That Will Reach the Lost*

Historians credit John Wesley as having the most significant ministry in reaching England and Colonial America with the Gospel in the eighteenth century. His influence continues to this day. The secret of his success was not in his methods, but in his personal disciplines. The following statement is attributed to him: "Do not seek after a ministry; anticipate the fruit of a disciplined life."

The Discipline of Prayer: Reaching the lost must begin with prayer. Jesus said to His disciples [lit., "disciplined ones"], *"The harvest truly is plenteous, but the labourers are few. Pray ye therefore the Lord of the harvest, that he will send forth labourers into his harvest."*[139]

The purpose of prayer is to free those under the bondage of Satan. This requires that we wrestle against principalities and powers and the rulers of the darkness of this world.[140] It is inconceivable that we would wrestle against these forces in prayer and then join with them in trying to reach the lost.

God assures us that tremendous power is made available to those who learn how to pray fervently and effectually.[141] God also promises that those who learn the discipline of praying in secret will be rewarded openly. [142]

Every great movement in history of reaching the lost has been initiated and sustained with prayer that includes Christians getting right with the Lord, cleansing their lives of sin and worldliness, and then releasing the bondage of Satan over the unsaved. David said, *"Create in me a clean heart O God. . . . Then will I teach transgressors thy ways; and sinners shall be converted unto thee."*[143] Where is the emphasis on prayer in all the discussion of reaching the lost through rock music?

The Discipline of Fasting: Jesus taught His disciples the discipline of fasting and promised that those who fast in secret will be rewarded openly.[144] The vital relationship between fasting and reaching the lost is explained in Isaiah 58. Through fasting we *"loose the bands of wickedness, to undo the heavy burdens, and to let the oppressed go free, and . . . break every yoke."*[145]

The discipline of fasting involves denying the body the fulfillment of its normal appetites. It is opposite to the spirit of rock music, which promotes fulfilling the lust of the flesh.

When Jesus was confronted by a boy who was overcome with demonic powers, He healed him. Later His disciples asked why they were ineffective in the healing of the boy. Jesus explained, *". . . This kind goeth not out but by prayer and fasting."*[146]

6 *How Reaching the Lost God's Way Produces Good Fruit That Lasts*

In John 15, Christ instructed that true evangelism is marked by lasting results: *". . . I have . . . ordained you, that ye should go and bring forth fruit, **and that your fruit should remain**. . . ."*[147] Prior to this century, great revivals brought people to the Lord through a clear presentation of the Law. The vast majority of those who became believers grew in their walk with the Lord.

In recent years our focus has changed to "finding a better life." God is viewed as a benevolent source of happiness, success, and prosperity. As a result, converts have no real understanding of sin or of God's holiness, and when persecution comes, they are ashamed of the Gospel and return to their old ways of life.

One of the analogies God uses to explain salvation is birth. As children develop, they take on the characteristics of their parents. Similarly, those who are won to Christ through preaching will revere preaching. Those who are brought to salvation through Bible teaching will tend to make that an important part of their Christian life.

George Mueller was brought to Christ through a prayer meeting, and he became one of the great men of prayer in history. What kind of heritage are we giving those who are won to Christ through the sensual characteristics of rock music?

CASTING DOWN THE JUSTIFICATION THAT
"THE ROCK PERFORMERS ARE SINCERE"

1 *God's Law*	2 *God's Examples*	3 *God's Concepts*
• God always combines sincerity with qualities such as truth and love. *"Now therefore fear the Lord, and serve him in sincerity and in truth: and put away the gods which your fathers served...."* • Sincerity is also measured by how our actions affect the lives of others. *"That ye may be sincere and without offense till the day of Christ."*	• David was sincere when he organized a procession to bring the Ark to Jerusalem, but he copied the world's methods and experienced the judgment of God. • King Saul was sincere when he offered sacrifices, but his worship did not follow God's ways, and he received a rebuke from the prophet and judgment from God.	• Sincerity requires that ministry be done in a motive of giving, not getting. *"Feed the flock of God ... not for filthy lucre, but of a ready mind."* • Making personal profit in the house of the Lord was abhorrent to Christ. The moneychangers claimed to help God's people, but God called them *"a den of thieves."*

1 *How God's Law Requires Truth Along With Sincerity*

Whenever the word *sincerity* is used in the Bible, it is always in the context of other character qualities such as **truth** and **love**. Notice the following verses:

- *"Now therefore fear the Lord, and serve him in **sincerity** and in **truth**...."*[148]
- *"Now therefore, if ye have done **truly** and **sincerely**.... If ye then have dealt **truly** and **sincerely** ... then rejoice."*[149]
- *"Grace be with all them that **love** our Lord Jesus Christ in **sincerity**."*[150]
- *"In all things shewing thyself a pattern of good works: in doctrine showing **uncorruptness, gravity, sincerity, sound speech** that cannot be condemned...."*[151]
- *"... I pray that your **love** may abound yet more and more in knowledge and in all **judgment**: That ye may approve things that are excellent; that ye may be **sincere** and without offence till the day of Christ."*[152]

- *"Your glorying is not good. Know ye not that a little leaven leaveneth the whole lump? Purge out, therefore, the old leaven . . . with the unleavened bread of **sincerity** and **truth**."*[153]
- *"For our rejoicing is this, the testimony of our conscience, that in **simplicity** and **Godly sincerity**, not with fleshly wisdom, but by the grace of God, we have had our conversation in the world, and more abundantly to you-ward."*[154] (The Greek word for *simplicity* means "generosity; singlemindedness; selflessness.")

To claim that rock music is honorable because the performers are sincere is not only an incomplete evaluation, but it contains other difficulties as well. The Word of God states that *"the heart is deceitful above all things, and desperately wicked: who can know it?"*[155]

In addition to the Scripture which requires more than just sincerity, it is important to realize that the "Christian rock" performers are better judges of their own sincerity than those who listen to their music. In personal interviews with several of the performers, they have acknowledged the double standard that exists in their personal lives and in their public performances.[156]

2 *How God's Examples Reject the Idea That Sincerity Makes Music Right*

Because the testimonies of the Lord are sure, making wise the simple, it is important to go to them for examples of how service to the Lord requires more than sincerity to be right.

King David was certainly sincere when he tried to bring the Ark of God to Jerusalem in a grand procession of praise, music, and dancing. Nevertheless, tragedy resulted, because he used a method that he borrowed from the world, and the procession ended abruptly in death and anger.[157]

David had gathered the nation of Israel together in order to bring the sacred Ark of the Covenant up to Jerusalem. He had it placed on a cart drawn by a team of oxen. As the procession made its way along the road, the people sang and praised the Lord. Then something unexpected happened. At one point the oxen stumbled, and the Ark began to slip. Instinctively, one of the men reached out his hand to steady it.

Standard Publishing, Bible Art Series, Cincinnati

Even though David was sincere, the method he used in worship violated the Word of God and brought swift destruction.

The man's action was a sincere attempt to protect the Ark; however, in so doing, he violated strict instructions of God that the Ark was not to be touched. Immediate judgment came as God struck the man dead, and David then became angry. The procession ended, and the Ark was left in a nearby house.

David had gotten his ideas from the Philistines. They had used a cart drawn by oxen to determine whether God had brought plagues to their cities.[158] God confirmed His message to the Philistines through this method; however, when David used the same method, God was greatly displeased.

The Law of God gave clear instruction that the Ark was to be supported by poles and carried on the shoulders of four priests.[159] At a later time, David used this Scriptural method and successfully brought the Ark the rest of the way to Jerusalem.

David could have argued that there was no Scripture specifically *against* using a cart, and it only seemed appropriate to use contemporary methods to draw people to worship. Nevertheless, these arguments would not have brought life to the man who had perished, nor would they have resolved the disillusionment of the people upon their worship ending in judgment.

Prior to David, King Saul had also demonstrated sincerity in his worship when he offered sacrifices to God before going out to battle. However, God was displeased with his sacrifices because of his disobedience. Therefore, God cut off Saul from the throne of Israel.[160]

3 *How the Concepts of God Expose the Ineffectiveness of Sincerity Alone*

The word *sincere* comes from the two Latin words *sine* and *cera*, which literally mean, "without wax." The expression "without wax" refers to a custom in pottery making. The expert potters would use only the best clay for their pots, and if they found any pebbles in the clay, they would start over again.

Those who used inferior clay would use wax to fill in any resulting pock marks after firing and then paint over it. When the buyer would put the pots in the fire for cooking, the wax would melt and run out. Thus the expert pottery makers would put on the bottoms of their pots *sine cera* ("without wax").

The Concept of Insincerity:

When rock musicians take the world's music and replace the lyrics with Christian words, it is like offering the world a vessel that contains things of which they are not aware. This practice constitutes insincerity, because it is an imitation of the real thing. Some Christians may respect "Christian rock" music, but most non-Christians view it as an imitation.

The Concept of Greed:

Doré

Are the "music changers" of our day any different from the money-changers of Jesus' day?

God condemns those who minister with motives of gain. Those in ministry are commanded to *"feed the flock of God . . . not for filthy lucre, but of a ready mind."*[161]

Christ was particularly harsh with the moneychangers in the Temple. They could have claimed to be sincere in trying to help the people carry out their sacrifices.

However, Jesus drove them out with the statement, *". . . Take these things hence; make not my Father's house an house of merchandise."*[162]

When "Christian rock" performers turn the church into a place of merchandise and the proceeds go to them personally, would they not fall under the same classification?

The Concept of Negligence:

The owners of a dairy company were very sincere in their desire to serve the public with quality milk products, but one day a salmonella outbreak occurred, and hundreds of people were infected by this dairy's milk. The plant was immediately shut down and an investigation was begun.

Health officials discovered that some equipment had not been thoroughly washed, and because of it, the milk became contaminated. Lawsuits began to pile up against the company, and a judge ruled that even though the company did not willfully infect people, it was, nonetheless, guilty of negligence. Today this company is bankrupt and out of business.

The *sincere* promoters of "Christian rock" music may claim that there are thousands of people who are helped by their music, but the time has come for them to recognize that there are also thousands of us young people who are being damaged by this music.

There is no question about the concern of our nation to protect the physical health of its people. There should be an even greater concern by the Church to protect the spiritual and moral health of its members.

When churches use rock music to attract teenagers, and immoral young people begin to attend the church youth groups, the church is guilty of negligence for not warning the Christians in the youth group who are not prepared for the seductive tactics of immoral and street-wise teenagers.

The Concept of Conspiracy:

The Fifth Commandment states: *"Honour thy father and thy mother: that thy days may be long upon the land. . . ."*[163] This command is repeated in the New Testament: *"Honour thy father and mother; which is the first commandment with promise; That it may be well with thee, and thou mayest live long on the earth."*[164]

It is a known fact that many of our parents do not want us to listen to "Christian rock" music. If "Christian rock" performers were really sincere, they would urge us to obey our parents in this matter. Instead, those who promote this music teach us how to stand up for our rights and listen to our music, regardless of what our parents think.

When Christian youth magazines teach us how to get around our parents and listen to rock music, they are guilty of conspiracy against the God-given authority and responsibility of our parents.[165] They are also damaging the most basic institution for the stability of any society and are thereby guilty of conspiracy against the nation. Most of all, they are guilty of conspiracy against the Law of God.

A sincere performer would not produce music that he knows is damaging to any listener. He would at least put on the label a clear message such as: **"Warning: It is damaging to your future to purchase this music or listen to it, if your parents are not in full agreement with it."**

The Concept of Contributing to Delinquency:

Every state in America has laws to protect minors from those that would encourage them in any way to be delinquent. Based on the testimony of thousands of young people, "Christian rock" performers have encouraged young people to engage in an addiction which has led many to acts of delinquency.

CONTRIBUTING TO THE DELINQUENCY OF A MINOR

Any person who knowingly or willfully causes, aids, or encourages any boy or girl to be a delinquent child or who knowingly or willfully does acts which directly tend to render any such child so delinquent is guilty of the Class A misdemeanor of contributing to the delinquency of children.

720 ILCS Illinois Compiled Statutes 130/2A
"Contributing to the delinquency of children," 1993

HOW IS ROCK MUSIC RELATED TO JUVENILE DELINQUENCY?

A study of rock music is not complete without the recognition of its clear relationship to rebellion, drugs, immorality, and the occult. The connection between these destructive behaviors begins with alienation from parents, then association with others who are alienated from their parents, and finally a participation in activities that are promoted by the message or lyrics of the music.

This relationship was also identified by a committee of the American Medical Association and reported in the *Journal of the American Medical Association*. Here is a report of that article:

AMA LINKS DRUGS, IMMORALITY, AND ROCK 'N' ROLL

"'Doctors should be alert to the listening habits of young patients as a clue to their emotional health, because fascination with rock 'n' roll, especially heavy metal music, may be associated with drug use, premarital sex and satanic rites,' a committee of the American Medical Association said.

"'At the very least, commitment to a rock subculture is symptomatic of adolescent alienation,' the AMA's Group on Science and Technology said in its report, 'Adolescents and Their Music,' published by the *Journal of the American Medical Association*.

"The AMA committee reported that 'the average teenager listens to 10,400 hours of rock music during the years between the 7th and 12th grades, and music surpasses television as an influence in teenagers' lives. While TV viewing often is supervised by parents, music is largely uncensored,' the committee said.

"'As an important agent of adolescent socialization, however, the negative messages of rock music should not be dismissed,' the committee said.

"The committee cited '. . . evidence linking involvement in rock culture with low school achievement, drugs, sexual activity, and even satanic activities.'

"The committee expressed special concern about . . . heavy metal rock and music videos.

"'The violent and sexual content of the video images are disturbing to many,' the committee said.

"'. . . A study found that 7th and 10th graders, after watching one hour of music videos, were more likely to approve of premarital sex than was a control group of adolescents.'"

Chicago Sun-Times, September 15, 1989

The legal question is, "Are Christian rock performers aware that their music has an addictive effect upon the listeners? Have they stopped to consider what causes thousands of listeners in their audiences to lose personal inhibitions and allow the music to control their actions with screaming, dancing, and a continuing insatiable desire for the rock beat?"

These performers would be quick to claim that they do not *cause* the unlawful actions of young people. However, the law is concerned with a wider scope of responsibility. The question of the law is, "Do these performers do anything to *contribute* to factors which encourage young people to become delinquent?"

HOW THE ROCK BEAT CREATES AN ADDICTION

Explained by a Psychiatrist

"One of the most powerfully addicting substances is something we carry with us in our own bodies. **It is our adrenaline.** When this substance is 'used' under the circumstances God intended, it is lifesaving and causes no urge to re-indulge. However, we are able to 'control' the release of this substance by choosing various activities which our defense mechanisms interpret as dangerous.

The Release of Adrenaline to Create a High

"Have you ever wondered why people pay such enormous sums to bungee-jump or to play video games excessively? When we choose to place ourselves under simulated attack situations, our bodies move into the 'fight-or-flight' response, releasing adrenaline into the blood.

"The heart pounds, eyes dilate, thoughts race, breathing quickens, muscles tense, and blood is shifted to the muscles. We are now ready to fight for our lives or run desperately for shelter. However, there is no one to fight or to run from. This situation causes a 'high' which feels exhilarating as long as we believe ourselves to be in control.

"This sense of control is the great lie of addictions. The god we create and control to give us a sense of worth, strength, and security turns on us. The servant god becomes a monster which overpowers us.

"I have seen addictions to adrenaline in veterans who turned to crime to repeat the 'highs' they had learned to enjoy in Vietnam. Others steal what they do not need, start fights over any protest, drive recklessly, spend all their time in an endless search for excitement, etc.

The Functions of Rock in Releasing Adrenaline

"One of the most powerful releases of the fight-or-flight adrenaline high is music which is discordant in its beat or chords. Good music follows exact mathematical rules, which cause the mind to feel comforted, encouraged, and 'safe.' Musicians have found that when they go against these rules, the listener experiences an addicting high.

"Like unscrupulous 'diet' doctors who addicted their clients to amphetamines to ensure their continued dependence, musicians know that discordant music sells and sells. As in all addictions, victims become tolerant. The same music that once created a pleasant tingle of excitement no longer satisfies. The music must become more jarring, louder, and more discordant. One starts with soft rock, then rock 'n' roll, then on up to heavy metal music.

Music Is a Stronger Addiction Than Alcohol or Cocaine

"With the teens and adults I have worked with, I find music addiction to be far more entrenched than alcohol or cocaine. I think this is in part due to society's acceptance of this behavior. Cocaine was once available over the counter in a 10 percent solution for hemorrhoids. Many people became addicted, and only slowly did society realize the devastation such addiction brought.

"Among the addictive characteristics I see in patients are: unhealthy curiosity ('what's so wrong?'); indulgence, even when they know their authorities disapprove; growing tolerance; ensuring their supply; making an exciting control game out of getting around parents' monitoring, saying, 'You had *your* music which *your* parents didn't understand, I have *mine*'; finding fault with authorities ('who are *you* to tell me what to do?'); talking about rights rather than responsibilities; claiming they could quit if they wanted to; and withdrawal from family relationships into fantasy relationships with a musician they'll never even see and certainly never have a healthy relationship with.

"When they see their preoccupation causing trouble, they try to 'go on the wagon' but never ask for help in quitting, so they fail. Like a pornographic addict claiming smut helps his marriage by making up for his wife's shortcomings, hard music addicts add 'good' lyrics, trying to make up for the failure of healthy music to give a high.

"If, in fact, such music were good, yet it offended 'weaker' brethren, a non-addict would drop the indulgence without a problem. However, addicts not only cling to their habit, but they attack those brethren whom they offend.

"Another characteristic of addiction is its power to consume all one's time and attention. They never ask what good is being displaced by the music. I have never known a person who listens to such music to regularly fast or pray. They never share verses they have memorized. They may show emotional affirmation of God, yet have no will for personal discipline.

"As other addicts, they only discuss their addiction to 'yes, but' the other person, rather than consider the danger. In addition to the adrenaline high, hard music is addicting because it drowns out thought. No library in the country would play this music in order to improve concentration.

"I have also noticed something interesting in patients who experience hallucinations. If they play classical music, they can ignore the voices and concentrate on the task before them. If they listen to hard music, they drown out the voices, but can't do anything else.

"I am impressed with how youth leaders adopt the approach, 'If you can't change them, join them.' Like all addictions, the victims pressure others to be quiet or to join in.

Understanding Mood Crashes

"I have also noted mood swings in all adrenaline addicts, including hard music addicts. It is normal after a fight-or-flight response to have a recuperation phase, even when one has had a venting of the energy building up. When the response has no energetic outlet, the high lasts longer, but is followed by a mood crash. The addict's solution is to try to stay high. This high cannot be maintained, but rather the longer the high, the deeper the crash.

"Many addicts affirm that the music actually calms them and they feel better. This is similar to a nicotine addict who claims that smoking calms him. Even after a cigarette, he is more anxious than he would have been if he had never smoked.

"Still the cigarette seems to calm because it reduces the withdrawal temporarily. Anti-anxiety drugs often do the same thing. They lose their beneficial effect, but now the person is anxious and must take the pills, because to quit is to be yet more anxious. It is the same with the music. Adrenaline addicts go into withdrawal or become immersed in the available music. They then get some 'relief' from listening, but no pleasure.

"I have found both despair and a tolerance of dangerous activities in music-adrenaline addicts. Danger can produce the same high, and the high feels similar to the music high. Thus the danger feels familiar—even comfortable. The brain system designed to protect from danger now leads into danger.

The Gradual Development of Addiction

"It has always been hard to connect causes and effects in medicine. The effects of addictions are slow, insidious, and hard to detect. When we add to this a willful blindness because we don't want to be involved with personal discipline, let alone place disciplines upon our young people, there is little hope of discovering the truth. However, God is not mocked: what we sow, we reap.[166] I have yet to see any good come from this music.

"Even if some permanent good could come from it, there is still the Russian roulette principle. If only one out of nine social drinkers becomes an alcoholic, what business do we have taking a one-in-nine risk? Such risks in medicine would be immoral. Would we put a gun with one bullet and nine chambers to our head and shoot? Would we then pass it around the group?

"The same applies to rock music. Maybe only one in ten is destroyed by full addictions and the rest suffer only lukewarmness and mediocrity. Still, what an indictment to the person who contributes to an environment which destroys his brother!"

—Verle L. Bell, M.D., Psychiatrist
Pastor, St. Paul Bible Church, Chicago, Illinois

Note: The same addiction that takes place in the lives of those who listen to rock music also occurs in the lives of those who perform it. This factor explains why the music of many "Christian rock" artists began with mild, contemporary music but gradually changed to a harder and harder rock beat.

How the Rock Beat of "Sincere Musicians" Affected the Heartbeat of a Susceptible Teen

The following report was written by the parents of seventeen-year-old Debbie, based on her experience at the Bremerton Naval Hospital on April 14, 1992:

"We have a seventeen-year-old daughter who recently had surgery to remove a benign tumor from her right index finger.

"In the middle of the surgery, the nurse came running down from the operating room to ask me if our daughter had ever had heart problems. She really never let me answer before she tried to assure me not to panic, although the heart monitor indicated dangerous heart problems.

"The doctors planned an EKG after the surgery. I wondered if the Lord had allowed the lump to grow on her finger so we could discover the heart problem before it became too serious.

"About 45 minutes later, the doctors and nurses wheeled our daughter into the recovery room where I was, and they were all laughing. They explained that as soon as Debbie's headset clicked off, her heart rhythm as revealed by the monitor went back to normal. They also said they were sending these details to a national safety board for review.

"Our daughter was listening to a 'Christian rock' tape called 'Beyond Belief' as she was in surgery. The staff in the operating room all agreed that what happened was 'beyond belief.'

"It is also interesting that just two days before the surgery, we had advised our daughter to listen to traditional Christian music, but she didn't."

—Mr. and Mrs. Tom Boyd, Washington

Upon learning of this incident, an obstetrician/gynecologist at another hospital noted similar evidences of increased heart activity in children in the womb when the mother listened to rock music. Additional tests are being conducted to further verify these findings.

WHAT CONSTITUTES LEGAL RESPONSIBILITY FOR CONTRIBUTING TO DELINQUENCY?

The Indiana law on contributing to the delinquency of a minor states that, "A person eighteen (18) years of age or older who knowingly or intentionally encourages, aids, induces, or causes a person under eighteen (18) years of age to commit an act of delinquency as defined by 16 31/6/4/1 commits contributing to delinquency."

The Factor of Prior Knowledge

It may be that rock performers and rock promoters have missed the obvious fact that their music has been addictive to us. If this happens to be the case, it is our purpose through this book and other publications containing our testimonies[167] to put all these parties on notice.

The Factors of Encouraging, Aiding, Inducing, or Causing

There is no question that those who promote rock music are guilty of all these factors. The addiction from the music separates us from our consciences, our parents, our inhibitions, and our moral standards. The natural result is that we will "commit acts of delinquency."

The Factor of Contributing to Existing Delinquency

It is not a valid defense to allege that a juvenile was already a delinquent as evidenced by prior actions. In *Davidson v. State*, 233 N. E. 2d 173 (1968), the defendant was convicted of contributing to the delinquency of a minor by causing her to desert the home of her parents and become involved in immorality. The defendant in this case asserted that he did not contribute to the delinquency of the girl because she was already a delinquent and had committed previous immoral acts.

The court held that the statute on juvenile delinquency is for the protection of minor children in our society, and the legislature has seen fit to protect children from vicious, immoral acts of older people. Even though those children may have been guilty of previous delinquent acts, it is the desire of the legislature to aid them and protect them from a continuation of a state of delinquency. It is no justification, therefore, for an adult to argue that because a minor is already a delinquent, there is no wrong in 'contributing' further to such delinquency.

In the case above, even though the minor involved was guilty of previous immorality, additional immoral acts with the appellant constituted 'contributing' to the minor's delinquency.

Angela (20) is one of thousands who have given similar testimonies of being drawn into rock addiction and wrong activities through music in the church.

A Serious Warning To Churches That Allow or Promote "Christian Rock" Music

"When I was twelve, I began attending youth choir at church. Up until then, I agreed with my parents that rock music was wrong. However, as I was exposed to it in church, my senses were dulled, and I began to accept certain styles of 'Christian' music, still believing *secular* rock was wrong.

"Before long, I was exposed to secular rock by my friends. I couldn't tell the difference between this music and the music I was hearing at church. The words were different, but I didn't think the words in secular music were always bad.

"I began listening to this music more and more. I saved up enough money to buy a headset so I could listen to this music without my parents knowing.

"At first, I just listened to 'Christian rock' and soft secular rock, but that quickly progressed to heavy metal rock and no Christian music—except on Sundays.

"I wore my headset constantly, except when I was in the car, then I turned on the stereo. If I was riding with my parents, I took my headset with me, even for short trips around town. If

I was in my room, I closed the door and played my stereo quietly. If my parents were gone, I turned it up full blast.

"I always had the volume on my headset turned up between seven and ten. It just seemed that I couldn't hear it if it was any quieter. I was addicted. I just couldn't get enough.

"Through all of this, my spiritual growth went on a rapid decline. I had shut everyone else out of my life, except those that listened to my music. I shut out the two most important spiritual leaders that God had given me—my parents. Even worse than that, I shut out God. I began telling Him that I didn't want anything to do with Him. I didn't read my Bible, didn't pray, and didn't want to go to church.

"The only input I had in my life was my rock music. Satan had a firm grip on my life. All of this climaxed one summer after I had just turned fourteen when I attempted suicide. When my attempt failed, I realized I needed to make some changes.

"I tried to rebuild my relationship with God, but my spiritual senses were so dulled that I didn't even realize what was hindering that relationship. When I was sixteen, I decided to give up secular music, but that didn't improve things very much. At the same time, I began dating a young man whose life dream was to own and operate his own radio station that played continuous contemporary Christian music.

"I supported that dream, still believing the lie: 'If we had more contemporary Christian music available to our young people, they wouldn't get messed up with that secular stuff.' My boyfriend had racks of C.D.'s on his wall.

"My parents urged me to give my music over to God. I assured them that I had; besides, I only listened to the Christian stuff now. I argued that I wouldn't make them listen to it, it was *my* music, God doesn't work on everyone in the same ways, etc.

"However, when I was seventeen, God began to work in my life. I realized that my parents were probably right. They had me read *Ten Reasons Why the Rock Beat Is Evil in Any Form.*[168] I couldn't argue with anything in it. I knew I was wrong, but I had to make a choice. I had to choose between God and the life I was then living (my music, my boyfriend, and my rebellion).

"On October 12, 1990, I had a spiritual 'knock-down, drag-out' fight with God. Praise the Lord—He won! That day I prayed a prayer, and I had no concept of how much it would impact me. I told God that I didn't really understand everything, but gave my music to Him. If nothing else, listening to rock was rebellion against my parents, and rebellion is as the sin of witchcraft.

"I asked God to restore a 'new and right spirit within me' and show me what was wrong. He did just that. I felt as if chains had fallen off me. When I hear music today that I used to listen to, I am horrified. I must have grieved God's heart so much!

"It breaks my heart to see other Christians follow the same path I did. Just as I was, they are more committed to their music than they are to God. I praise the Lord for the renewed spirit and senses He has given me, and I plead with you not to promote 'Christian rock' or to make the same mistake I did."

Angela Brandel, Idaho

How Do Product-Liability Laws Apply to Those Who Produce and Sell Rock Music?

Because of the testimonies of users and the damages and injuries incurred by rock addiction, those who produce or sell rock or rap music should be aware of product-liability laws.

Product-liability laws protect consumers from harmful or defective products or products that do not sufficiently warn the user of unseen dangers. These laws also provide for compensation to those who have been harmed by such products.

If rock music is purchased by someone who is not aware that it has an addictive nature, and if that person becomes addicted to rock music by listening to it and damage occurs as a result of his addiction, those who produced or sold the music should be liable for the damage that occurred to the user.

There are three requirements for a plaintiff to establish liability on the producers or distributors of a product: 1) There was action, whether intentional or negligent, taken by the producers or distributors of the product which made the product more dangerous than the consumer was aware. 2) An injury occurred to a user of the product. 3) There is a direct link between the injury incurred and the product itself (causation).

(William P. Statsky, Torts: Personal Injury Litigation 494–503, 1982)

The addictive rock beat that has been added to music has caused psychological and physical harm to many young people as a direct result of drugs, immorality, or alienation from parents. Producers or distributors of rock music should place warning labels on their tapes and compact discs telling of the dangers of addiction by listening to their music.

One might argue that food can be addictive—this is true. Thus, God puts warnings in the Bible about the dangers of overeating. (See Proverbs 23:1–3, 21.)

A Wise Answer to a Promoter of "Christian Rock" Music

When an article entitled "What Does God's Favorite Music Sound Like?" appeared in a trusted Christian magazine, twenty-three-year-old Wendy Griffin wrote the following response to the author.

"Your editorial in the January 1993 edition of your magazine prompted me to write you. Respectfully, I must tell you that you are wrong about the Striving for Excellence[169] program. Allow me to tell you how music has affected me, so you will understand my position.

"I was raised in a Christian home and made a profession of faith at the age of five. Until I graduated from high school, I had a strong faith in God, and I was committed to living a Godly life. However, my choice of music dramatically changed my life, and the consequences of my rebellion have limited my ability to attain the Godliness to which I aspired.

"I was introduced to rock music when I began keeping a nursery for a local aerobics class. I began to listen to music that my parents did not allow in our home. The more I listened to this music, the more I wanted to listen to it, and the more I desired the various kinds of rock music available.

"Against my parents' wishes, I moved away to attend college. I discovered more and more artists whose music I liked. I had begun by listening to 'soft' rock music but was led into harder and harder stuff, until I became what you might call a 'subdued headbanger.'

"I began flirting with occult activities, especially astrology and mind-control techniques. I found that I could alter my mood easily if I put the right cassette into the stereo—I could make myself sad, angry, or manic (never happy). I could completely lose my mind, if I wanted to.

"As I continued to listen to this music, I was led ever deeper into rebellion against my parents and the values that they had taught me. By the time I graduated from college, I was mired in anger, drinking, depression, self-hatred, sexual promiscuity, eating disorders, and suicidal thoughts. I continued to flirt with the occult and with 'soft-core' pornography. My grades plummeted, and nothing could motivate me to do anything—nothing but music. Rock music ruled my life.

"I am grateful for the people and events that God used to bring me back to Himself. Financial difficulties forced me to return home, and my parents asked me not to listen to rock music anymore. They said that the sustained tension it created was making me irritable and difficult to get along with. They told me that my music was affecting my spiritual, mental, and physical health.

"Then I discovered the principles presented in Striving for Excellence. My notes from college verified this material, including an outline of basic music theory and composition. This outline gave me good, factual reasons to reverse my listening habits.

"By the world's standards, the music that I listened to was quite innocent. By the standards applied in your magazine, the music consisted of 'good overall picks.' However, when I gained a more complete understanding of music, I realized that the music with which I had saturated my life had damaged me greatly. Many people had warned me that rock music was harmful and dangerous, but I chose to disregard their warnings. It was not until I stopped listening to rock music that I began to comprehend the effects that it had on me—and its power over me.

"When I stopped listening to rock music, I was amazed to find my mind revitalized. I could memorize and meditate on Scripture again. I could concentrate on whatever task I was doing, so my job performance improved dramatically. My father remarked that my eyes had lost their dull look and were beginning to shine with alertness and joy. He also noted that my countenance had softened.

"I found myself less anxious as the sinful oppression under which I had labored for years was lifted. I began to develop an intimate relationship with my Savior. All these wonderful things did not happen overnight. It has taken over a year to get where I am, and I have a long way to go, but it was the principles explained in Striving for Excellence that got me back on the right path.

"I would now like to address some of the specific statements in your editorial. I have a great deal of experience in music, as I have been studying it for the better part of fifteen years. I minored in music in college, and have studied music history, music theory, and musical performance. I am a student of piano, flute, and voice.

"You state that the approach taken by Striving for Excellence is oppressive; your implication being that it is legalistic and rigid. Music, as with all other facets of life, is governed by certain rules. Some of the most important rules in music are those which balance harmonies and rhythms with melody.

"Judicious infringement of these rules in music enhances it (adds excitement), much as adding a little salt to food enhances its flavor. However, just as too much salt in food is poisonous to the body, too much 'excitement' in music is poisonous to the soul.

"Rock music combines the two most detrimental and dangerous forces in musical composition: driving backbeat and unbalanced, chaotic harmonies. These characteristics affect the listener's heartbeat and respiration. More significantly, they are tools with which a musician or performer can manipulate the emotions and behavior of his audience.

"Rock music is not a wise choice of listening material for a Christian. In practice, I have not found the principles set forth in Striving for Excellence to be either legalistic or oppressive. I have found them inexpressively liberating. I wish I had known of them ten years ago, before I made so many mistakes."

Wendy Vanessa Griffin, Tennessee

What About Martin Luther's Use of Contemporary Music?

One of the rationalizations we previously used to justify "Christian rock" was, "What about Martin Luther? He used the secular music of his day, so why can't we do the same?"

This rationalization breaks down under both logic and research:

- As believers, we are to pattern our lives after Christ, not after men.

- The folk music of Martin Luther's day was melodious. Therefore, to use this in an analogy is not only inaccurate but deceptive.

Martin Luther's purpose in creating hymns was "That the words of the Scriptures should be placed in the mouth of every member of the congregation."[170]

- Much of the folk music from which Martin Luther drew his melodies was religious folk music of the pre-Reformation period. Some of these songs had been sung as early as the ninth century.

- Of the melodies in Martin Luther's thirty-seven chorales, fifteen were composed by Martin Luther himself, thirteen came from Latin hymns, four were from German religious folk songs, two had originally been religious pilgrim songs, two were of unknown origin, and only one came directly from a secular folk song.[171]

The one secular song came from a popular folk song, "I Arrived From an Alien Country" and was first used in a chorale as a melody for Martin Luther's famous Christmas hymn for children, "From Heaven on High, I Come to You."

This song appeared in Martin Luther's first hymnal in 1535 but was replaced by an original tune in his 1539 hymnal. Historians believe that Martin Luther discarded the secular tune after only a short time because of people's associating it with its previous words.[172]

- The goal of Martin Luther in music was to replace the world's music, not to duplicate it. He used four-part harmony because he wanted to attract youth away from the world's songs.[173]

HOW TO BE A CONQUEROR

1 Be Truthful About Symptoms of Addiction.

Read the ten characteristics of addiction on page 5, and acknowledge those that apply to you. If you consistently listen to any music with a rock beat, you should be alert for addiction.

2 Regain Surrendered "Ground."

Trace tormentors such as depression, fear, and lust to times when you went to bed angry, lusted after evil things, or committed immoral acts. Follow the steps on pages 30 and 31.

3 Pull Down "Strongholds" With Truth.

Each rock song has built false presuppositions in your mind, will, and emotions from which you will make wrong decisions. These false ideas must be identified and replaced with the truth of God's way of thinking. Study pages 37 to 94.

4 Replace Rock With Melodious Music.

Cleanse your heart and home of any music that has the rock beat (a heavy or subtle beat on beats two and four in four-four time—also called *backbeat*). In melodious music, the emphasis is on beats one and three (in four-four time). Another sensual technique in rock music is called *scooping*, and it involves vocalists starting just below pitch and sliding up to the pitch. If you cannot locate melodious music, we will be happy to help you. Write to us at **Triumphant Music • Box One • Oak Brook, IL 60522-3001**.

5 Brighten the Lives of Others.

Thousands of young people who have conquered rock addiction want to encourage you to maintain your freedom. Unprecedented opportunities for those whose lives demonstrate victory are documented in a new video entitled *How the Light of the Eyes Opens Nations to the Truth*. Be a part of making history!

This video is available for $25 (plus $4 shipping) from IBLP Publications • Box One • Oak Brook, IL 60522-3001 or by calling (708) 323-9800.

NOTES

1. *Taber's Cyclopedic Medical Dictionary*, 16th Ed., F.A. Davis Co., ©1989, p. 36.
2. *Webster's Ninth New Collegiate Dictionary*, Merriam-Webster, Inc., ©1989, p. 55.
3. This ATIA survey consisted of 10 questions answered by young people and affirmed by a parent.
4. Ibid.
5. John 4:23
6. II Kings 17:16–18
7. Galatians 5:17
8. I Corinthians 6:12
9. I Corinthians 9:27
10. Alexander Pope
11. 720 ILCS Illinois Compiled Statutes–130/2A– "Contributing to the Delinquency of Children."
12. Ephesians 4:27
13. II Corinthians 10:4–5
14. Matthew 7:22–23
15. John 6:38; John 12:49
16. Ephesians 4:27
17. I John 1:9
18. Colossians 2:13–15
19. Revelation 12:11
20. Psalm 23:3
21. Proverbs 28:13
22. James 1:21
23. Romans 13:14
24. Acts 19:19
25. John 15:13
26. Psalm 19:7
27. Mark 12:30–31
28. Romans 3:20
29. Psalm 19:7
30. I Corinthians 10:11
31. I Corinthians 10:13
32. II Timothy 2:15
33. Psalm 19:8
34. I Samuel 30:24
35. I Samuel 30:25
36. I Timothy 5:18; Deuteronomy 25:4
37. I Timothy 5:17–18
38. Psalm 19:8
39. Matthew 22:35–40
40. Proverbs 6:20–23
41. Luke 11:34
42. Matthew 5:16
43. Psalm 19:9
44. Matthew 6:1–18
45. Joshua 1:8; Psalm 1:2–3
46. Proverbs 22:4
47. Psalm 19:9
48. I Kings 3:28
49. Proverbs 15:3
50. Ibid.
51. II Corinthians 5:10
52. Ecclesiastes 12:13
53. I Kings 22:42–43
54. Genesis 1:31
55. Acts 15:29
56. Exodus 20:14
57. James 4:4
58. Michael Ventura, "Hear That Long Snake Moan," *Whole Earth Review*, Spring 1987, pp. 28–43, and Summer 1987, pp. 82–92. *Warning:* There is danger in studying the details of false religions. (See Deuteronomy 12:30.)
59-70. Ibid.
71. Ephesians 4:27
72. Revelation 12:11
73. James 4:7
74. Romans 13:14
75. Colossians 3:16; Luke 11:24–26
76. II Timothy 2:15
77. Matthew 6:18
78. II Timothy 2:16
79. Matthew 4:1–11
80. Matthew 16:21–23
81. Genesis 11:7–9
82. Ephesians 4:29
83. John 12:49
84. Matthew 16:22–23
85. Acts 17:11
86. Exodus 20:16
87. Proverbs 19:5, 9; see also James 3:10
88. Ezekiel 44:23–24
89. II Corinthians 6:16–17
90. Ephesians 5:11
91. Judges 2:2
92. Psalm 106:34–41
93. Exodus 20:12
94. Ephesians 6:2–3
95. Malachi 4:6
96. Mark 1:23–25
97. Acts 16:16–18
98. Numbers 22:22
99. Numbers 25:1–18
100. Deuteronomy 22:10
101. II Corinthians 6:14–16
102. Revelation 3:15–16
103. I Peter 5:8–9
104. I Corinthians 14:8
105. Matthew 7:15
106. John 10:4–5
107. I Samuel 15:23
108. Matthew 16:23
109. Hebrews 13:4
110. Colossians 2:8
111. I Corinthians 14:8
112. II Corinthians 10:5
113. Proverbs 4:23
114. Philippians 4:13
115. II Timothy 2:15
116. Colossians 3:16
117. II Corinthians 1:21
118. Galatians 1:8
119. II Corinthians 4:2
120. Ephesians 5:19
121. Romans 14:7–21
122. I Corinthians 8:9–12
123. Matthew 7:9
124. Galatians 6:10
125. Matthew 25:31–34
126. I Timothy 3:2–7
127. Acts 16:25. The Greek word translated "praises" in KJV is *humnéo*.
128. Matthew 5:16, 6:22
129. Acts 5:13–14
130. I Samuel 16:23
131. Acts 19:13–20
132. Galatians 3:24

133. I Corinthians 15:10

134. Titus 2:11–12

135. Jude 3–4

136. Ephesians 4:30; I Thessalonians 5:19

137. Colossians 2:8

138. Acts 20:29

139. Matthew 9:37–38

140. Ephesians 6:12

141. James 5:16

142. Matthew 6:6

143. Psalm 51:10, 13

144. Matthew 6:18

145. Isaiah 58:6

146. Matthew 17:21

147. John 15:16

148. Joshua 24:14

149. Judges 9:16

150. Ephesians 6:24

151. Titus 2:7–8

152. Philippians 1:9–10

153. I Corinthians 5:6–8

154. II Corinthians 1:12

155. Jeremiah 17:9

156. Examples of quotations can be found in *CCM* magazine, and a list is printed in *The Battle for Christian Music*, by Tim Fisher (Greenville, SC: Sacred Music Services, 1992), pp. 123–125.

157. II Samuel 6:1–11; I Chronicles 13:1–14

158. I Samuel 6:1–16

159. I Chronicles 15:15; Exodus 25:14

160. I Samuel 15:23–35

161. I Peter 5:2

162. John 2:16

163. Exodus 20:12

164. Ephesians 6:2–3

165. One such article was "Shake Down at Home," by Nancy B. Bayne, *TQ*, January 1990, p. 32. We are grateful for the editors of this magazine, who heard our appeal regarding this article and agreed not to publish any further such articles.

166. Galatians 6:7–8

167. *What the Bible has to say about "Contemporary Christian" Music (Ten Scriptural Reasons Why the Rock Beat Is Evil in Any Form)* and *Notice of Complaint Against the Unrecognized Enemy in the Church*

168. Ibid. (IBLP publication)

169. Instructional material on music evaluation (IBLP publication)

170. Erik Routley, *Church Music & Theology* (London: SCM Press, 1959), p. 61

171. W.B. Squire, "Luther," *Grove's Dictionary of Music and Musicians*, V, (New York: St. Martin's Press, 1955), p. 446; Martin Luther, "An Order of Mass and Communion," trans. Paul Strodach, *Liturgy & Hymns*, Vol. LIII, *Luther's Works* (Phila.: Fortress Press, 1965), p. 36; and Martin Luther, Preface/Geystliche Gesangk Buchleyn," *Works of Martin Luther*, ed./ trans., Paul Strodach (Phila.: Muhlenberg Press, 1932), p. 284.

172. Ulrich S. Leupold, "Learning from Luther," *J of Church Music*, Vol. VIII, Jul/Aug 1966, p. 3; Paul Nettl, *Luther and Music*, trans. Best/Wood (Phila.: Muhlenberg Press, 1948), p. 48.

173. Friedrich Blume, *Protestant Church Music* (New York: W.W. Norton & Co., 1974), p. 10.

The Reward
of Conquering

THE ADDICT
OF ROCK MUSIC:

BRIGHT EYES

Unprecedented opportunities are now open to young people who demonstrate God's Light to the world. (See page 95.)

"Let your light so shine before men, that they may see your good works, and glorify your Father which is in heaven. . . . The light of the body is the eye . . ." (Matthew 5:16; 6:22)